# Divination with Stones

## A Beginner's Guide to Lithomancy

### Divination for Beginners
#### Book Five

## Monique Joiner Siedlak

oshunpublications.com

# DIVINATION WITH STONES

## A Beginner's Guide to Lithomancy

## MONIQUE JOINER SIEDLAK

Divination with Stones: A Beginner's Guide to Lithomancy © Copyright 2023 by Monique Joiner Siedlak

ISBN 978-1-961362-06-2 (Paperback)

ISBN 978-1-961362-07-9 (Hardback)

ISBN 978-1-961362-02-4 (eBook)

**All rights reserved**

The content contained within this book may not be reproduced, duplicated or transmitted without direct written permission from the author or the publisher.

Under no circumstances will any blame or legal responsibility be held against the publisher, or author, for any damages, reparation, or monetary loss due to the information contained within this book, either directly or indirectly.

**Legal Notice**

This book is copyright protected. It is only for personal use. You cannot amend, distribute, sell, use, quote or paraphrase any part, or the content within this book, without the consent of the author or publisher.

**Disclaimer Notice**

Please note the information contained within this document is for educational and entertainment purposes only. All effort has been executed to present accurate, up to date, reliable, complete information. No warranties of any kind are declared or implied. Readers acknowledge that the author is not engaged in the rendering of legal, financial, medical or professional advice. The content within this book has been derived from various sources. Please consult a licensed professional before attempting any techniques outlined in this book.

By reading this document, the reader agrees that under no circumstances is the author responsible for any losses, direct or indirect, that are incurred as a result of the use of the information contained within this document, including, but not limited to, errors, omissions, or inaccuracies.

**Cover Design by MJS**

Cover Image by VadimVasenin @depositphotos.com

**Published by Oshun Publications**

9 Old Kings Road STE. 123 #1038; Palm Coast, FL 32137

www.oshunpublications.com

# More Books in the Series

**Divination Magic for Beginners**
Divination with Runes
Divination with Diloggún
Divination with Osteomancy
Divination with the Tarot
Divination with Stones

# Contents

| | |
|---|---|
| More Books in the Series | 1 |
| Also Available | 3 |
| Newsletter Signup | 5 |
| Introduction | 9 |
| 1. The Ancient Whisper of Stones | 13 |
| 2. Stone Signatures: More than Meets the Eye | 21 |
| 3. Your Stone, Your Story | 31 |
| 4. The Stone Spectrum | 37 |
| 5. Sanctuaries of Stone | 45 |
| 6. Formations of Fortune | 49 |
| 7. Harmonizing with the Hard | 59 |
| 8. Layouts: The Lithomancy Lexicon | 65 |
| 9. Mastering the Mystic Mineral | 71 |
| 10. The Ethical Edifice | 79 |
| 11. Living the Lithomancy Legacy | 85 |
| 12. Interpreting the Stone Meanings | 91 |
| 13. Creating Your Own Lithomancy Set: A Personal Touch to Divination | 99 |
| 14. The Power of the Lithomancy Chart | 103 |
| 15. Stones in the Stream of Life | 109 |
| Conclusion | 119 |
| References | 125 |
| About the Author | 129 |
| More Books by Monique | 131 |

# Introduction

Would you believe me if I told you there was a way to decipher the past, present, and future from simple rocks and stones? Within each of us is the innate ability to tap into foretelling. Some of you are connected deeply to your conscious state and will already be able to tap into this on demand. Others of you are sitting on the edge of a cliff, looking over and waiting to fly. Knowing that you have the potential but need help activating it. A deep connection to self opens up a world of spiritual gifts and abilities that can help you in your life and business. We can tap into a learning path from our ancestors by harnessing relationships, abundance, and companies. This has been lost over the decades as we have evolved and moved to a more media-controlled way of living and receiving information. Being drip fed slowly over time, where true wisdom has been fortuitously diluted.

Where does your wisdom come from? What is your source of knowledge? And my guess is if you're reading this, you know that you are already thinking outside of societal norms and teachings. Or you're a seasoned spiritual practitioner seeking to add another string to your bow. Either way, what you're about to learn will blow your mind and expand your cognitive state into the past, present, and future as we shift your level of understanding and transcend ordinary perception. Are you ready?

But before we set off on our journey, what is spiritualism? Over the years, spirituality has grown as people look for a way to make sense of life and for self-exploration. Countless books have been written on what it means to be conscious and awake at this time on Earth. We see reams of spiritual coaches and mentors helping people find their truth, claiming to help with manifestation and abundance. We see others embracing this support and living not only in their dreams but in their soul purpose too. Is it real? Or is it all just noise?

Well, this is familiar, and spirituality has been around for thousands of years, even before the time of Jesus Christ, the most notable figure in the history of faith. Over the centuries, spirituality acquired different names and filtered into different countries and religious practices. But the heart of spiritualism remains the same across every ritual, tradition, or religion. It believes in a higher power and a divine source. This hasn't changed over time, and, for the most part, spirituality has beautiful effects on people's lives.

The belief that the soul transcends into another realm is also at the core of spirituality. That there is more than just our physical body and soul continues onto a higher realm. Is this true? Well, that depends on your belief system.

But where does that leave us when seeing into the future? Is this magic? Magic is open to interpretation too. However, those that claim to know what magic is will tell you that it is connected with energy and metaphysical power. That same energy is found everywhere, in physical form, on our Earth. This is the energy of the stones, rocks, crystals, and minerals around us. They form the structure of the Earth from its core up to its mantle and in the hills, mines, rocks, and mountains all around us.

Rocks emit a vibrational frequency, and spiritualists believe those frequencies can help us see into the future when we use them in divination. Is this a safe and well-balanced way of viewing ourselves and our lives? Yes, it is. Because it gives us the opportunity for clarity in our words, self-reflection on our mistakes, and personal growth in making better decisions for the weeks ahead.

Welcome to the world of divination. Welcome to Lithomancy. The ancient practice of looking at the past, present, and future using oracle stones. In the spiritual field, the mind-expanding words we use to talk about mystical practices sets us apart from other belief systems. But don't let that divert your attention. Stay with me as we embark on a journey into another dimension of reality but in a very current and practical way.

Your voyage with me is understanding lithomancy, how it works, and how you can incorporate stone divination into your life and business. So, please close your eyes, take a few deep breaths, and slowly sink back into the past to see how these prophetic stones came to play a massive part in our way of living.

## Chapter 1

# The Ancient Whisper of Stones

Can you imagine being able to see into the future? Would you believe me if I told you it was possible and that all you needed to do was awaken and connect to your spiritual abilities? Well, it's true. But before we begin foretelling with stones, we must first unpack its unique history. Then, your practice will hold a distinctive richness and quality that overrides other spiritual practitioners and give you an edge.

Once you fully understand the culture behind this art, the symbolism of your work with divination may change. Understanding how symbols were interpreted in the past will help you translate what the stones tell you today. We can get very superficial readings when we use stone divination without knowing its history or origin. And I know you want to be the best spiritual counselor you can be!

Looking at Lithomancy throughout time lets us see how it's changed or misinterpreted. This gives you some vital clues to misjudgments you've made or inaccurate or blocked readings. Everything you learn here is value-packed and will seal your knowledge as expertise.

And lastly, if we continue to breathe life into this esteemed tradition, we must pay homage to its roots, celebrating and learning from them. Noticing how our ancestors changed aspects of the tradition to enhance and develop the prophetic practice while keeping its roots planted in its diverse and mystical soil.

## Unveiling Lithomancy

Lithomancy is also called stone divination. A lithomancy practitioner that is an expert in this craft is called a diviner or lithomancer. Many old pagan terms, where the word lithomancy comes from, have changed in recent years to clarify sacred spiritual arts like this and make them easier to understand by people like you and me. Having obscure or too traditional terminology sometimes prevents people from learning more about these beautiful, enriching spiritual practices. This allows us to absorb the details of foretelling with stones a lot easier!

So, what is foretelling with stones? Well, simply put, it's a way of seeing into the forthcoming months ahead by looking at a reading featuring ourselves and the important things in our lives. The stones are cast and read alongside planetary activity and our spiritual self. We can use a reading to look into the past, present, or future and see about three months at a time.

This enables us to notice if there will be periods when we should take action or if there is any planetary activity that would prevent us from making changes in our lives. There is nothing wrong with looking into the future. It is a magical process gifted to all who know how to tap into their divine intuition. And it's important to stress that all future events are changeable and not set in stone. This is true, no matter what anyone tells you.

So, consider lithomancy a map or a framework to plan future events. One where you can confirm your feelings, questions, thoughts, and doubts in love, life, work, finance, family, and spirit. We can combine all the important factors of daily living into a stone reading to give us confidence or reaffirm ideas on a particular subject.

Lithomancy allows us to look into the past. Sometimes we

make decisions that, with hindsight, we would change. When we look at a stone casting and combine these with events in the future, we can explain or understand why we took a specific action or felt a particular way. Trying to find logic in life is something that we all do from a very young age. And due to the downfall of the family structure in recent years, spirituality has grown in response to the demand for guidance and support where society has failed. It's no surprise that this faith continues to grow in popularity.

Lithomancy is the sacred art of reading the future using stones. These can be stones, crystals, rocks, minerals, or pebbles. And each stone has a meaning attached to it. So, when the stones are dropped, cast, or thrown by the diviner, a pattern created by the stones can be interpreted, and this is where the fun begins!

The meanings given to the stones are done by the intuition of the practitioner, the lithomancer. If you are the stone diviner, you can follow the guidelines from ancient traditions or cultures or solely use your divine intuition. It's all up to you!

Casting the stones in a special area or circle will create a formation you can read. Looking at particular areas of interest in your or your client's life. You can ask the stones questions and look at how they land, about one another, to tell a story or read the map about the road ahead.

Lithomancy enhances the areas of personal growth and self-exploration. As humans, we desperately seek the answers to everything in life. This allows us to serve others ethically. We are not here to predict the future but to help guide and understand future conditions for the benefit of our clients. We can hold space for them while they make decisions and positive moves.

Lithomancy gives its users clarity and helps guide them toward achieving the most genuine desires. It's not witchcraft or hocus-pocus. It's not religion, dogma, or God. It is tapping into the energies of the frequencies of this Earth, provided effortlessly by the stones and our divine intuition, to seek a better way forward through daily living. It helps explain the ups and downs that life throws at us and allows us to better understand. It's a beautiful, nourishing people-centered tradition to seek the best in life. Always think of it simply as the ultimate map!

## Tracing the Veins of History

The history and origins of stone divination travel far back in time. And what's interesting is that as soon as man could write, evidence of lithomancy was revealed. There are 3 main periods where stone divination held cultural significance, with its roots also burrowing into Asian and Indigenous tribal cultures

- Ancient Mesopotamia
- Ancient Greece and Rome
- Medieval Europe

Let's embark on our first journey of discovery into the history and origins of stone divination. What you discover here will profoundly affect how you interpret your reading of the magical stones.

**Mesopotamian Mystics**

Mesopotamia is often called the "cradle of civilization," the Mesopotamians were the first to discover and create writing over 2000 years ago. It is no surprise that evidence of stone divination was found here, too, detailed on the clay tablets that the Mesopotamian scholars created to write on; found in what is now known as modern-day Iraq.

The Babylonian divination methods were also famous in this region in the ancient world. Dr. Marie Besnier claims that *"...for the Mesopotamians, the world is ruled by a complex system of correspondences between signs and human life that relates all events to one another."* They believed in a holistic view of life, and these signs were understood as messages from the gods.

Mesopotamian magic was very much part of everyday living. It was steeped in culture in ancient Iraq and the imperial peripheries of Syria, Anatolia, and Iran. Omens, delivered from many signs, including stone divination, would provide a guide by which the Mesopotamian people would live by. And the Mesopotamian magicians of this time would be responsible for foretelling and interpreting medicine, science, literary, religious, and magical parts of daily life. For the ancient people of Mesopotamia, magic wasn't just a way of living; it was in their blood.

Records of these findings, detailed on clay tablets dating from the first millennium BC, show that this deep tradition had a pervasive presence in everyday experiences. It was not just a practice accessed solely for spiritual alignment or well-being.

**Grecian and Roman Revelations**

While the history of lithomancy remains vague throughout the ages, we can see evidence of stone divination in ancient Greece and Rome, dating back to around 500 BC.

The art of stone casting was mainly used in astragalomancy, also known as cubomancy or astragyromancy. Astragaloi, known as knucklebones, were predominantly used for foretelling the future. The ancient peoples often struggled with many concepts of life under the umbrella of health and illness, such as death, childbirth, and disease. Divination methods were used to help make sense of the future and aided decision-making in uncertain daily situations. Only a little is known or recorded, but we do know from fragmented resources of ancient archaeological artifacts and written accounts that it played a societal role in the culture of this period.

**Medieval Mosaic**

With the origins of lithomancy deeply anchored in pagan practice, it's hard to believe that it still retained a presence in medieval Europe around 476 AD, when Christian beliefs dominated societies across The Old Continent.

At this time, it had become less of a daily practice and more of a way to tell the future and harness spirituality. Nevertheless, it was still widely used. As it was now frowned upon and considered sorcery, diviners were not famous people; however, the use of their magical service was still sought-after.

There are no reams of extensive historical data that we can rely upon. But we do know from grimoires and historical manuscripts that lithomancy was common in many different parts of Europe and played a role in unassociated cultures.

Elements of stone divination evolved and were used in connection with astrology and conjunction with divination tools. We began to see the casting of stones in different arrangements, with divination boards, cloths used in readings, and the stones positioned in different spaces to record their symbolism.

Lithomancy, after this time, lessened in popularity over the years. What we know as Tarot replaced stone divination. Tarot cards are still widely used by spiritual foretellers and healers today.

The myths that stem from Lithomancy remain fascinating. Such as Photius, the head of the Christian Church in Constantinople, writing about the practice sometime after 801 AD, and Helen of Troy, seeing the destruction and downfall of the famous Troy empire in a stone reading.

Lithomancy's strong and remarkable past intrigues us. It draws us in, confirming and cementing itself as part of our cultural heritage. But how does it now fit into our modern-day society?

## Modern-day Marvels of Lithomancy

Considering what we know about the history and origins of Lithomancy, it seems strange to now think of stone divination as something to be savored in only the spiritual or supernatural realms. In our human need to make sense of everything and attach logic, scientific reasoning, and justification to only the things we can see and that are tangible, we lose pieces of our cultural heritage. And sometimes, our pagan roots in parts are unimaginable and dark, but they remain our roots, nonetheless.

Looking at lithomancy with a very modern-day, practical

outlook, we can start to refer to it as guidance. And that guidance may take shape in helping you to make decisions, find reasoning or hope in a particular situation or relationship; it may provide answers to something you need clarity on or be a means to connecting to a spiritual or higher realm.

And stones also look pretty hanging around your neck or sparkling on a shelf! Whatever the reason, stone divination has a varied presence in life today, such as in:

- Crystal Healing
- Jewelry
- Spiritual Practices and Rituals
- Home Décor

Their use is divergent and opposing but shows that we have this undeniable connection to stones, their energy, their meaning, and their exquisite beauty.

When it comes to the practice itself, there are many ways people practice stone divination, and the rules and meanings that align with it are often variable and unique to each practitioner.

This ancient art has also moved away from its geographical origins. It is now kept alive predominantly in Western society, especially since the rise in spirituality amongst English-speaking nations. Practices like this are common in health and well-being settings. They are on their way to being normalized when reducing stress, amplifying energy, or as part of healing therapy.

So, with all this in mind, we're going to delve into the traditional yet modern-day practice to see how you can use this ancient art of foretelling the future and implement it into your life or your business. Are you ready to make a start and unravel the details of your spiritual practice?

## Chapter 2

# Stone Signatures: More than Meets the Eye

The key to a successful reading lies in the meaning of the stones. Once you understand this, stone divination will feel like a breeze. For a lithomancy practitioner, interpretation is the whole kit and caboodle. It unlocks the secret prophecies to your stone divination readings. In this chapter, we will uncover the symbolism of the stones and how they played a part in ancient culture and traditions; to help you become a wizard (or witch) of this practice!

### Embedded Emblems: Stone Symbolism

Oh, my divine essence! Now we're getting into the meat and bones of lithomancy! Get ready for excitement as you learn about the stones and their meaning. There are primarily two sets of stones; planetary based on astrology and personal stones.

**Cosmic Stones: The Planetary Ambassadors**

**Sun:** The role of the Sun is significant, and this stone rules, literally! It acts as a commander of the zodiac sign, Leo, and in astrology, the Fifth House. The Sun stone governs how we present ourselves to the world and controls aspects of us, such as life force and ego. The Sun behaves like a beating heart in the solar system. It also relates to personal power and confidence. It is connected with influential people, particularly the dominant male role model in families, government workers, and world leaders. This stone helps us to shine and show the strength of who we are to the world. The Sun's cycle has an important role, too, as it takes an entire year to cycle through the zodiac signs. When you think of this stone, think of energy, vibrancy, life force, and a powerhouse for illuminating the way!

**Moon:** Reflecting nature, the Moon stone is the opposite of the Sun. Equally powerful, but a complete contrast. Like the mother, the Moon represents our family's dominant female role model. It has nurturing qualities and a repeated cycle, taking twenty-eight days to venture around the zodiac and the Sun. This stone behaves like a looking glass. It shows us what's happening inside us emotionally and speaks to our passion, curiosity, and dreams. The Moon stone has a deep connection to home, so, unsurprisingly, it's linked with the zodiac sign Cancer. It's also tied to the Forth House and reflects the past. When you think of the Moon stone, think of feminine energy, change, and reflection.

**Mercury:** This stone relates to intelligence, logical thought, humor, and our brain. Mercury represents speed, reflected in its speedy orbit around the Sun, only taking eighty-eight days. Due to its fast-moving nature, Mercury shows up in the zodiac four times a year, always giving us the opportunity for growth and learning. However, Mercury can also make us fidgety or anxious if we cannot move. Its movement is also connected to travel and communication, enabling us to learn and take that into the world to share with others. In the zodiac, it's connected to Gemini and Virgo and the Third and Sixth Houses. When considering gender-neutral Mercury, consider being curious, intelligent, teaching, speaking, and world travel.

**Venus:** Well, well, well, imagine Venus, fiery and feminine, a powerhouse of fuel and love; what a glorious sight! This is our happiness and relationship stone, focusing on love and radiant beauty. Venus is a slow-moving planet taking two hundred and twenty-five days to orbit the Sun. The Venus stone adds depth to our relationships, harnessing romantic love and strengthening the bond between sisters and daughters, bringing a ton of feminine energy into our family settings. The Venus stone is connected to peace, friendship, and the nice things in life, even our material belongings! It is tied to the zodiac signs Taurus and Libra and the Second and Seventh Houses. When you think of Venus, think of power, love, art, nature, and the slow-moving, deep, and caring side of love.

**Mars:** We can all envision Mars as a warrior with powerful male energy. Attributes of the Mars stone are adventure, strength, and strong vibrational frequency. Mars has aspects of male energy, such as confidence, strength, adventure, toughness, and resilience. Despite its partnership with energy, it's a slow-moving planet, taking six hundred and eighty-seven days to go around the Sun. Mars likes intensity and can cause a little upset here and there with accidents and tension in relationships. However, it makes us courageous and ready for change. Bring in the new with Mars! It is linked to the zodiac signs, Aries and Scorpio and the First and Eighth Houses. When considering Mars, imagine fighting, winning, strength, courage, and bravery.

**Jupiter:** This stone reflects wisdom and is our second gender-neutral planet. Jupiter is the largest planet in the solar system. It reflects our performance by helping us to see the biggest and best in everything. The Jupiter stone, like Mercury, makes us feel intelligent and hopeful for the future. Jupiter is also connected to education and learning, and there is a feeling of abundance and luck with this stone's vibration. It is a super slow planet taking twelve years to go around the Sun, linked to the zodiac signs Sagittarius and Pisces and the Ninth and Twelfth Houses. When you think of the Jupiter stone, think of opportunity, luck, abundance, and wisdom!

**Saturn:** Welcome to the house of rules and authority because Saturn likes to play a strict game. Another planet to harness learning, but this time reflecting limits and administering restrictions and seriousness. The Saturn stone will teach you about hard work to achieve your goals. Saturn will enforce responsibility and show you that all actions have consequences! This disciplinarian stone takes twenty-nine years to orbit the Sun while transmitting wise and slow frequencies. It's connected to Aquarius and Capricorn and the Tenth and Eleventh houses. When you think of Saturn, think of the strict teacher who wants you to score highly on a test without cheating, no rule-breaking, limitations, and wisdom.

**Uranus:** Calling all rebels, this is the planet stone to call in the revolution! When Uranus shows up, everybody is happy. Uranus is cool and the epitome of breaking the rules, supporting the freedom to be who you want and change. This is the individual stone, calling in all things quirky and unusual, helping us to celebrate our individuality. The Uranus stone is related to new ideas, inspiration, and metamorphosis. Another gender-neutral planet, but a big game-changer, Uranus makes its mark in the world and takes eighty-four years to go around the Sun. Uranus brings big things into the open and is connected to Aquarius and the Eleventh House. When you think of Uranus, think of a change catalyst, freedom to be whom you want, and transformation like you've never seen before!

**Neptune:** This planet stone is like an enigma, full of mystery and magic. Neptune harnesses our imagination and allows us to dream. Neptune is a caring stone, making us susceptible and aware of others' emotions. It draws the empath in us and gives us the gift of consideration of the world. Neptune wants us to help others. It's a female planet moving super slowly around the Sun, one hundred and sixty-five years, to be precise! When considering Neptune, consider femininity, dreams, imagination, and compassion.

**Pluto:** Tapping into your subconscious and deep thoughts lies the Pluto stone. And this is also a slow-moving stone, orbiting the Sun every two hundred and forty-eight years, capable of uncovering deeply hidden matters. This stone identifies significant changes and areas of transformation; it can reveal things we don't know are there and, subsequently, make huge life transitions. It is connected to Scorpio and the Eighth House. When you think of Pluto, think of uncovering the mystery, femininity, rebirth, transcending, transformation, and superhero-style power!

**Inner Mirrors: Personal Stones**

**Life Stone:** This stone behaves like a reflection of how you see yourself in this lifetime. The life stone connects us to our journey and is like a mirror. It helps us focus on what we want in this current existence and makes our client the center of attention.

**Luck Stone:** This is a stone that has special significance. It is generally believed that luck happens by chance. However, this stone shows us that it is shaped by our choices and the good thoughts and deeds we act upon.

**Love Stone:** This stone is so important to us. It focuses on relationships and our emotional attachment to those we love and adore. Family, friends, and lovers are all part of the wisdom of this stone.

**Magic Stone:** This stone really should be called the time stone! It helps us see when there is an excellent time to do something special and work out when we are in the flow. It works beautifully alongside the life stone to give us an idea if we are moving too fast, too slow, or in the right place at the right time. Just like a magical clock!

**Places Stone:** This stone represents any of the places in our lives. This can be home, work, or even places we travel to. It allows us to see these places and what's working well or needs change. This stone is all about the personal places linked to your client.

**Commitment Stone:** This stone does what it says; it tells us all about our commitments. These can range from paperwork to legal matters or even promises we have made. If the love stone connects with the commitment stone, it also tells us about our love ties!

Both the planet stone and personal stones need to be chosen by you. You can select from crystals and gemstones to shells and rocks. Use your intuition, but if you need a starting point, here are some ideas of the types you can use to get started. We'll go into further depth about the frequencies and characteristics of these stones in the next chapter:

- Sun
- Moon
- Mercury
- Venus
- Mars
- Jupiter
- Saturn
- Uranus
- Neptune
- Life
- Luck
- Love
- Magic
- Places
- Commitment

## The Geological Glossary

What can geology tell us about the link between Earth and the spiritual realm? The geological characteristics of lithomancy stones act as a direct link between these dominions. In the astrological plane, the planets, and the solar system, multi-dimensions can also be called in. The shapes, clusters, and colors represent the universe and the tie between all things. Let's explore geology and oneness.

While we have scattered access to the history of lithomancy, secrets of its geological characteristics tell important tales about stone divination. Some would argue that lithomancy is all hocus-pocus. But it remains a fact that the study of the reading of rocks is regarded as a geological investigation, a scientific study. And stone interpretation is recorded way back to the first millennium

BC when the first writing was created on clay tablets in Mesopotamia.

Subsequently, we know the importance and significance of stone reading in any form. This is evident in the archaeological findings of the first recorded information, what we now call writing. People were advancing, learning, and using this mineral-based transmission to unravel their ideas and next steps to help them make better daily decisions. It is no surprise that if stone and clay tablets were used to write on, these same stones could be scattered to see if patterns were present, in a rudimentary way, to foretell the future.

Interestingly, stones from different climates and origins hold different frequencies. These stones become a sacred part of a stone divination ritual. Depending on your lithomancy tradition, they may have a significant purpose or provide insight.

Alongside these frequencies is the energetical vibration from the stone. And again, these will be different depending on where the stone has been mined. The mineral composition will vary from one county to another, and each place will have its own cultural or religious ties to the energetical composition of that stone.

These are all fascinating parts of stone divination to ponder when choosing your stones. Always make decisions based on your intuition and the practice you are most aligned with. No one knows better than you when it comes to our divination practice.

## Spirit Stones: Their Sacred Footprints

Stones, as a link to the spiritual realm, have been part of every significant spiritual practice and religion since records began. But why? Well, stones have a special significance in several ways. If we travel far back, we used stones in most ritualist ceremonies. And when we talk about ceremonies here, we will include religious ones, as at the core of every religion lies the deep roots of spirituality. This does not mean one practice is favored over the other.

These are simply pertinent examples we shouldn't ignore as a means to develop our understanding and further expand our minds into the many flavors of spirituality and its practices.

**Let's take a journey backward and see where stones were hailed as worthy parts of traditions:**

Firstly, stones and healing: as far back as we can see, stones have been used as healing tools due to the frequency they vibrate. This is evident in Native American history, where stones were physically laid onto the body to draw in energy and pull out unwanted vibrations. They are also present in Japanese Reiki to stimulate flow within the body. Chinese history shows us Feng Shui; rocks and minerals are placed in all kinds of areas of the home to promote flow. In India, the ancient Ayurveda art of using crystals to harness energy centers around the body is still practiced today. Stones and healing have a parallel symmetry that has remained constant throughout the centuries and transcends time and cultures.

Secondly, stones and intention or prayer: even though there is fierce denial from many Christian sects, the use of stones is present in many religions. According to one Christian denomination, The Annunciation Trust, states "You could carry a stone in your pocket or bag, and when you touch it remember to pray. Pray for whatever is on your mind then—and remember to thank God for his love. Is there something you want to ask the God or Goddess to forgive you for? Hold the stone and pray, ask the God or Goddess to forgive you, and allow the stone to drop gently into the water. Feel the weight of your sin washed away. Thank God for the insights you have received from holding your stone."

In Catholicism, we see rosary beads used for prayer or when asking God for forgiveness, yet the Vatican aggressively opposes using rocks and minerals, referring to them as a means to call in dark magic. This is untrue; every practice can be translated or perverted to suit evil ways or support public shaming of certain traditions.

We can also include Islam and the famous Black Stone, which

sits by the Kaaba. In the Holy Quran, gemstones such as emeralds, rubies, and jade are all mentioned as having healing properties. And not forgetting the prayer beads used in everyday Islam to keep count while speaking the repetitive glorifications of Allah's name.

In this same way, stones, minerals, rocks, and crystals are used in spiritual practices too. Holding a stone while making an intention has the same feel as prayer, just with a different name. Worry, or prayer stones, are present in Buddhism, and Hinduism brings in precious stones and crystals to connect with astrology.

In spiritualism, shamans use rocks and stones to call in the divine presence and for protection, much like Native American culture does. Chinese spiritualism, Feng Shui, uses stones to ward off evil presence and attract positive vibrations.

Crystals, precious and semi-precious stones, are used across all cultures, religions, and spiritual practices. We see and find them everywhere despite their sometimes being savage opposition about their role. Now, isn't that just divine? Now it's time for you to select YOUR stones.

## Chapter 3

# Your Stone, Your Story

There is next-level excitement when you start selecting your stones. The tiny embers of a flame begin to ignite into a blaze inside you. In contrast, the energy these vibrational rocks emit begins to call in your intuition. A huge learning curve sweeps you away, and your knowledge deepens and widens, enhancing your second sight. And as you progress with your understanding of this unique art, your connection develops too.

## The Pulse of Personal Connection

The role of personal connection in lithomancy is a game-changer because not all spiritual healers and practitioners are created equal. Diversity in the spiritual community is as colorful as a rainbow. Each wizard, witch, and warlock have unique spiritual abilities, and you will have too. With that in mind, all lithomancy readers are deeply diverse and may specialize in specific types of readings, such as love or fortune. Others may offer more holistic interpretations, looking at the bigger picture. Whatever type of reading you choose, your clairvoyant (and that could be you) has a personal connection with their stones. How they cast them will play a big role in explaining a reading.

**The way a lithomancer interprets the stones is personally influenced by many things:**

- **Symbolism:** lithomancy has a wide and varied history. Depending on which historical background is attached to that reading style, different stones will represent symbols.
- **Stone Energy:** your lithomancer will emit different energy depending on their vibrational frequency. Stone energy is amplified by the energy it's surrounded with, making energy alignment important.
- **Emotional Ties:** emotional connection to stones is strong, with some feelings being more significant than others. This type of energetical connection deepens and strengthens the meaning of the reading itself.
- **Mastery of Lithomancy:** experience and ownership are important in stone readings as they increase the accuracy of interpretation and elevate confidence and intuition in this art.
- **Deepen Enlightenment:** the stronger a personal connection gets to a set of stones, the more enlightenment the caster receives. We know that intuition deepens when we reach different levels of understanding. The same applies to the stones. The deeper we connect, the more enlightenment and wisdom we are open to and receive.

Your connection will also influence and affect the quality of the stones in this tapestry of ancient truth, so let your mind stay open and receptive. At the same time, we look at evaluating the quality of stones.

## The Quartz Qualities: Evaluating Stone Virtue

Your lithomancy stones' quality differs from shopping at Target and Chanel. There are three categories of stones you can source to present in your lithomancy castings

- Fake Stones
- Unethically Sourced Stones
- Ethically Sourced Stones

Working with crystals for many years, I have seen many stones come from various sources and countries. I know how to spot an inauthentic citrine that is heated-treated amethyst. Or moonstone that is too pearly, polished, shiny, and smooth to be real.

Now, as practitioners, we don't just stop using these stones when we have no alternative because they are, in fact, ubiquitous. You'll see them everywhere for sale, from spiritual fairs and high street stores to reputable crystal dealers. The simple fact that a crystal has a different composite or has been dug up under not-so-ideal conditions is part and parcel of the gemstone world.

We need to remember here that specific stones must be used as part of a ritual, which means sometimes, no other stone will replace its characteristics. But we can modify, add, or reduce the stone's energy to our readings and provide substitutes to a stone casting if we need to.

Being a reputable wizard or witch in this practice is all about knowledge. And we can tweak the process here and there if a problem arises, using our intuition as a guide.

Unethically sourced stones can carry negative energies. Suppose someone has gone under extreme pain or terror to retrieve a crystal. In that case, some of that energy will have transferred to the stone during the extraction process. Maybe life has been lost in the removal of the precious rock. This changes the stone's vibration; some crystals will continue to hold and transmit that negative vibration.

Ethically sourced stones will contain different energy. They will be radiating positive particles, having been extracted with love and care. This energy will also be inside the vibrational frequency emitted from the stone. You can see the vast difference here, and you need to do your homework regarding where you buy your rocks.

And before we close this conversation, don't forget that stones can be channeled with divine messages from your higher being or your angels and guides. They can be used in dark arts and contain curses or metaphysical parasites. Always be aware of where your stones come from, and cleanse them regularly and before use.

## Intention Stones: Crafting Your Quest

Intention is the sacred force of your higher self that will drive your every thought and word into action. So, now this is where your readings get interesting! Every client or reading you cast will have a specific intention. You may be interpreting the stones to discover the future of a relationship, a work promotion, or health and wealth matters, or your client's desire is to see into a window of time before embarking on a new path. Whatever the direction or subject matter of a lithomancy reading, there will always be a strong intention behind it.

Stones can easily be matched to intentions, and that's because, in every crystal, there is a vibration and frequency. Find similarities between the stone and the message you have been asked to deliver. You do not need to know vast information from your client, but you need to ask their intention. Let's take a few examples to see how this can give meaning to your hallowed truth ceremony:

- **Love or Relationships:** Rose quartz is a perfect choice to assist in readings where love, relationships, and self-love are tied into your client's intention. It radiates and amplifies the energy of love.
- **Wealth:** Citrine is an excellent choice for attracting what you deeply feel emotionally and manifest, particularly good with money or financial intentions. But a word of caution with this stone. If you have deep worries about something or a poor money mindset, citrine can attract more bad stuff instead!
- **Health:** Clear quartz is powerful for clearing energies and blocking damaging electromagnetic waves everywhere nowadays. This "master healer" would be a perfect place to start for a reading with a health or well-being objective.
- **Intuition:** If you are required to give a general lithomancy reading, you could use amethyst to enhance and deepen your intuitive power. This will open up and develop foresight and allow you to feel the divine message downloading rather than using your mind to decipher the sacred meaning.

Now the mud is clear on your divine selection of stones, and we've ramped up your enthusiasm to get your readings started, let's begin to choose the stones that will be perfect for your lithomancy practice.

## Chapter 4

## The Stone Spectrum

I know you've been dying to get here, and so have I! It feels like we're now getting to the meat and bones of stone divination. The world of practical steps is about to open up and unfold like a beautiful lotus on a lily pad. You can feel your psychic juices flowing; even my spirits and guides can sense your eagerness to push forward on your journey into foretelling with stones.

### Precious Paths: The Role of Gems

When we imagine stone readings, we envision sparkling gems and gleaming rocks in an array of exciting, vibrant colors, catching the light and pulsating with vibrating stone energy. But that is sometimes what the movies and TV would have us believe. Many stones are used in lithomancy, varying from wizard to witch, warlock to shaman! Although the role of both precious and semi-precious stones in divination is somewhat similar, so let's take a look at their overlapping aspects first:

Emotional attachment to your client: Your client may have a stone that has a unique meaning or emotional significance they want to bring to the reading and this could be any stone.

1. **Stone Symbolism:** A particular stone may symbolize healing or transformative energy, which may frame the details of your reading.
2. **Stone Energy:** Reading patterns is an essential part of lithomancy. The energy given from either type of stone is vital in providing clues to the outcome of the reading.
3. **Cultural or Historical Significance:** Any stone used historically or culturally may hold keys to unlocking the details of your reading, with either precious or semi-precious stones.
4. **Tradition:** Both types of stones have been used ritually over time. It's important and, some would say, sacred to continue this practice in the same way.

But while there are parallel roles for both precious and semi-precious stones, there are also notable differences:

1. **Aesthetics:** Precious and semi-precious stones can come in various colors, shapes, and sizes. Pretty, sparkling, colorful stones will add depth, fun, and enlightenment to a reading. And this can also be part and parcel of cultural and ritualistic significance.
2. **Ethics:** Stones that could be more pleasing to the eye may need to be wielded to make the stone reading accurate, far from fancy, but ethically correct and dedicated to the accuracy of the stone reading taking place.

Paying homage to the divine roots of this ancient pagan art will always outweigh the appearance of pretty gems. The practitioner's reputation, without exception, will be the most important characteristic upon delivering a reading.

Divination with Stones

## Common Crystals: The Everyday Enchanters

Now your head must be spinning with all the ideas of different stones and crystals you could use in your new, contemporary way of foreseeing events. So, where do you start? Before we engage with our psychic senses, it's worth noting that experts of lithomancy don't often divulge details of the exact stones they use during their readings. And here, we come back to the idea of personal stones containing special significance, perhaps to pull in a distinct emotion, release a unique vibrational quality, or stones that are married to a specific origin, culture, or trend.

However, that doesn't stop us from looking at some of the most common stones used in lithomancy, and as 16 are used, we'll cover all 16 of them here. Excited? So am I! Let's take a look at an overview of these exquisite minerals and some of their energetic, healing, and spiritual properties:

1. **Clear Quartz:** Clear quartz is well known as the master healer and one of the most powerful stones in the crystal kingdom. It has healing properties beyond compare, blocking electromagnetic waves and protecting energy. A stone that can be programmed and channeled and, interestingly, holds a program well.
2. **Citrine:** Citrine is well documented as the stone of abundance, especially financial abundance. But citrine has many more qualities; absorbing, transmuting, and grounding negative energies. Self-esteem, clarity, and confidence are elevated in citrine's presence, alongside removing energy blocks standing in your way. Personal power is harnessed, and this stone is a superpower when tackling depression, fear, and phobias. Physically, it helps energize and invigorate, helping you pack a punch of enthusiasm

for life, relieving symptoms of digestion and constipation, and improving circulation.
3. **Black Obsidian:** This creative stone helps with your journey into past lives. It encourages your true self to come forward even through time, so care should be taken with black obsidian. This mineral helps you manifest spiritual energies on Earth. Not a stone to be taken lightly.
4. **Labradorite:** The magic stone is black with glittery hues of mystery and incantation. A powerful psychic, spiritual stone to give you a deeper connection while protecting you. It enhances spiritual abilities, purpose and amplifies intuition. A protective stone, assisting transformation and easing emotions. Metabolism and hormones benefit from keeping this crystal in your periphery.
5. **Rose Quartz:** Rose quartz is the heart stone known as a crystal of love and love and suitable for all kinds of relationships. Its warmth attracts many souls while it heals wounds, calls in self-love, and connects you to your heart chakra. Beautifully protective and healing for your emotions. Its close connection to the heart makes it perfect for improving the circulatory system and reducing anxiety and stress.
6. **Selenite:** Selenite creates a link between the physical and spiritual worlds. If you want to amplify the energy of your stones, place them in a selenite bowl. Great for shifting energy blocks and bringing in cleansing, even with free radicals, as it's such an impressive purifier.
7. **Lapis Lazuli:** Lapis helps strengthen your third eye, opening up the possibility that it blends spiritual, emotional, physical, and mental aspects of you to harmonize your body from the inside out. A beautiful

blue stone that wards off depression and boosts immunity.

8. **Moonstone:** Hailed as the stone of new beginnings, Moonstone uniquely amplifies intuition and increases spiritual abilities. Sometimes known as the woman's stone or water stone, it activates the pineal gland for increased awareness and higher connection. Good for balancing emotions and calming hyperactivity.

9. **Carnelian:** you may have heard Carnelian referred to as the performer's stone. A stone of confidence and creativity. The unique qualities of Carnelian are courage, confidence, and inspiration, which drive ambition and determination. It works on both sides of the brain, bringing creativity and mental focus together. When coupled with rose quartz, it can harness its owner's passion and deep love. Physically, it can help balance your blood flow and spiritually works well with your root and sacral chakras to ground you into your life's purpose.

10. **Amethyst:** purple amethyst attracts peace and calm, balances emotions, and offers relaxation. It also relieves physical, psychological, and emotional pain, reduces bruising and swelling from injuries, and battles insomnia. Amethyst is a powerful healer for cleansing your aura and transmuting negative energy.

11. **Turquoise:** Turquoise has been a revered stone since ancient times. It offers protection, grounding, and strength. Spiritually, it bridges earthly and heavenly realms, enhancing intuition and meditation. It's known to align all chakras, fostering inner harmony. As a healer, Turquoise aids emotional balance and supports the immune system. Its calming energy dispels negativity and promotes self-realization.

12. **Bloodstone:** Bloodstone, often termed the 'stone of courage,' revitalizes both body and soul. Energetically,

it grounds and protects, fostering love and preventing negativity. Its healing attributes bolster the immune system and purify the blood, renowned for supporting vitality. Spiritually, Bloodstone stimulates dream activity and intuition, anchoring the heart chakra and renewing relationships.

13. **Sodalite:** Sodalite, the 'stone of insight,' fosters understanding and intuition. Energetically, it harmonizes imbalances, promoting inner peace. It balances the throat and third-eye chakras in healing, aiding communication and deepening perception. Spiritually, Sodalite encourages self-trust and introspection, guiding one towards a profound inner journey and spiritual growth.
14. **Tiger's Eye:** As the 'stone of protection,' radiates bold energy and confidence. Energetically, Tiger's Eye grounds while enhancing vitality. It balances the lower chakras for healing, aiding in discernment and clarity. Spiritually, Tiger's Eye fosters courage and resolves internal conflicts. Its golden rays inspire action and decision-making, while its earthy tones provide stability and reflection.
15. **Malachite:** Malachite, dubbed the 'transformation stone,' amplifies positive and negative energies, necessitating mindful use. Energetically, it offers protection, absorbing pollutants from the aura and body. In healing, it supports the heart, aiding emotional balance. Spiritually, Malachite reveals subconscious blocks, promoting personal growth. Its vibrant green swirls symbolize nature's regenerative power.
16. **Jasper**: Known as the Supreme Nurturer, offers grounding energies and emotional strength. Energetically, it stabilizes auras and shields against negativity. As a healer, Jasper sustains physical and

emotional well-being, supporting organs, and stress relief. Spiritually, it aligns chakras, facilitating shamanic journeys and dream recall. Its spectrum of colors mirrors Earth's majesty.

## Energies Etched in Eternity

Working in the spiritual space, you already know that intuition is essential to understanding divine messages, downloads, and spiritual guidance. You may have learned to turn on the tap to your higher self and instantly decipher intuitive messages from many energetical sources. And one of these sources is the stone's energy.

Energy radiates and pulsates from the Earth. Different energies emerge from different layers of rock, crust, and mantle. Each of these energies holds contrasting vibrations. Vibrations come from the mineral composition of the rock. When combined or aligned, different minerals create a rainbow of vibrations, all unique, complex, and divine.

Each vibration can be interpreted depending on its influence on culture, history, and origin. Over time, some rocks and minerals have claimed and retained their famous energetic characteristics. They've been celebrated for their ability to ground you, heal you, and call in spiritual abilities or abundance, and so on.

When a rock, stone, crystal, or mineral has passed through time, delivering consistently on its signature program, it's safe to say this energy is reliable and sustained. We can confidently bank on this stone to give us what it says on the tin.

But there is another aspect to understanding a stone's energy. And your distinctive intuition will guide you to interpret each stone. You may have experience using a mineral because you have channeled it with messages from your spiritual guides and ancestors. You may have encountered this stone being useful in specific cases. You may have first-hand knowledge of traditions, and different cultural rituals handed down over generations that others don't have access to.

Picture this: Now I know that citrine calls in abundance, but not many practitioners will tell you that citrine call in the abundance of anything the owner is feeling at that moment in time. So, if you're stressed about bills and amplified with citrine's energy, you could be calling in more and more bills! Don't be fearful of your intuition and knowledge. This is your unique skill and will set you apart from practitioners with less understanding and wisdom.

And this gently brings us to the cosmic and mystical energy of stones. Metaphysical properties can be part of crystals and stones. Does a spirit reside in your stone? Have you channeled it from your or your client's, angels and guides? Every one of these storylines will change the vibrancy of that rock.

Let's not forget the cosmic energy of the universe. Where does your stone originate, and has it been affected by astrology or the planets? Are there celestial bodies or star energy permeating your precious crystal? The Earth is one thing, but the universe's influence is another.

Look at a stone's energy holistically, with a well-rounded view, inviting your stones to be captivating, full of personal treasure, and wisdom from another realm. During a reading, this can help you bring practical advice into this moment in time in a pragmatic way to explain all the delicious ingredients of your lithomancy casting. Now you know what stones you can use, let's prepare to set up your sacred and bespoke stone reading space.

## Chapter 5

## Sanctuaries of Stone

You will never remember what someone said, but you will always remember how they made you feel. Body language, smell, first impressions, and the setting are all part of creating the right atmosphere and backdrop for your lithomancy readings. Let's get started!

### Ambiance of Auras

Firstly, make sure the space you've selected has the right energy. It should be free from any distractions or noise interrupting your divine messages. It should be a sacred space where you are free to think and feel about downloading information you are ready to receive.

Secondly, remember to cleanse the setting regularly and in between readings. Create a ritual for your readings, perhaps with a few candles or oils burning, or do what is sacred according to the history and terms of the practice you command. You may have an altar to place and rest your stones and cleanse them in a selenite bowl.

Lastly, your lithomancy environment should be comfortable. Do you need to remove your shoes to ground you with the Earth as you cast and interpret? Or does your client need to sit with you at a table, or do you prefer a different setting? Other questions will come to mind as you set up your space, helping you be flexible as you begin your practice and because you may want to make changes along the way.

All these factors are important to make your mastery of this shamanic art a holistic experience for your client and, more importantly, for you so you can execute the most accurate reading possible.

Now we'll learn how to arrange these precious stones to prepare you for your first reading!

## Stone Circles: Arranging Your Allies

Let the stones act as your guide in your lithomancy readings. It's time to tune into your intuition and let that be your higher self, be your lighthouse. There are two documented ways stones are arranged, strategic placement and tossing. Still, I am sure, as with many ancient traditions, other methods may remain a mystery.

The easiest way to connect with your intuition is through meditation. Meditating will allow you to see and feel where the stones need to be placed. You will receive divine messaging, hear words or instructions, or visualize where the stones should go. This part of lithomancy is unique because of many interpretations of shamanic art. You must feel into and find which version feels aligned with your spirituality and beliefs. You become the portal for the past, present, and future. There is no right or wrong, only your interpretation of the casting. Trust your sense of knowing and progressive wisdom.

Alternatively, you or your client can lightly toss the stones during a reading. We will go into more detail about this in the next chapter, but this arrangement of the stones gives a more energetic approach to the art. The spontaneity and vibration from the toss pay respect and connect to the many ways lithomancy was practiced by different cultures. And in this way, your reading is not strategic or planned, and none can accuse you of falsifying or mapping out the message.

Whichever way you decide to arrange your lithomancy stones, make sure it feels right to you. Our pineal gland and third eye deactivation have lessened over the years. We rely more heavily on our other senses to provide us with information in our daily lives. However, our spiritual awareness sits just below the surface, waiting for its activation by complete trust and connection to ourselves.

## Purifying the Portal

There are many ways to cleanse the vibrations in your space before dimming the lights, calling in your divine energy, and slipping into your intuitive state!

First things first, keep your stone casting area clean and tidy. It's not unusual for us spiritual beings to be intensely creative, which sometimes makes us messy! Keep electronics away from your reading sphere, as electromagnetic waves alter the frequency of your stones and can interfere with interpretation. A glaringly obvious notion but often ignored by many.

Cleanse with essential oils, especially those that open up a spiritual pathway, such as vetivert, frankincense, and myrrh, as they are all beneficial to deep relaxation and opening your mind. If a particular oil was used in your historical lithomancy tradition, include it in your purifying ceremony. Remember, everything about your ritual is unique, sacred, and important.

Cleansing with sage or smudging goes back in time and is easy and quick to perform, especially between readings. It cuts through energy like a knife and transmutes negative resonance. Remember to speak your intention while smudging; ensuring your space is free from human and mystical vibrations for your next reading.

Sprinkle rock salt into the corners of your room, in doorways, windowsills, or other openings to stop negative forces from entering. You can also sprinkle a little on your altar too if you're using one (and a good idea to use one too).

Crystal cleansing is also a beautifully aesthetic way to purify a space. Clear quartz and selenite are your go-to crystals to fight energies, neutralize an unfavorable aura, and settle disturbed vibes.

Regular cleaning of this space is so pleasing in many ways, and it will also help you to push unwanted energy away from your physical being and remain connected, balanced, and in flow.

Excited to set up your space? I bet you are! And I'm guessing you're even more excited to learn how to read the stones. It's time. Let's go!

## Chapter 6

## Formations of Fortune

Reading the stones may feel scary and complex, but it's not! Please take a deep breath, trust your intuition, and let's dive in, head first, into the sacred knowledge you're here to receive.

### First Principles of Stone Semantics

The beauty of stone interpretation is not to follow a set of instructions or documented resources of a scientific process. It's a hugely personal and intuitive art. No one can tell you that your reading is incorrect. The insight and wisdom received from the stones are based on your experience and connection with them. And many shamans, witches, wizards, and warlocks do this in several ways. Some can't even explain the process of receiving information; it can come in as sound, vision, or signs only visible to the practitioner.

At first, especially when starting, you may need more confidence in your abilities. But apply the rule, practice makes perfect, and practice, practice, practice! This will expand your knowledge of the stones and increase your ability to feel the answers or messages flowing from the minerals.

Watch out for patterns. There will always be similarities and differences in where the stones fall. Two or a cluster of stones sometimes position themselves together. What does this tell you? Stones may fall outside of your reading area. Does this mean this stone is irrelevant to your reading, or does it have a different explanation altogether? Some spiritualists may enforce their code of lithomancy on you, but none can tell you or teach you about your intuition. This divine force and tool will help you create the most accurate reading ability.

But to help you deliver these readings on tap, we must start by following the basic principles of stone formation reading guidelines. And these will help you to create a routine and ritual that you will memorize. Over time, this will become second nature, and you can turn on your intuition like a tap in this sacred space.

**We can begin to create a stone divination guide in the following order:**

**Cleanse Yourself**

You and your body must be free from conflicting energy and vibration. You can wash with water before casting your stones or smoke and smudge yourself with sage. Either option remains sacred to your practice and has the same clearing and neutralizing effect.

**Cleanse Your Lithomancy Space**

The same applies to your blessed lithomancy zone. Try to keep it free of electronics (which I know is hard but, all the same, remains doable!) to allow the environment to be unaffected by electromagnetic waves. These deeply affect how we feel and function, so they could have direct and adverse consequences on the stones themselves and the interpretation of your casting.

**Choose Your Stone Casting Area**

Your stone casting zone may change depending on which client you are reading for. Or you may have a casting area significant to your divination tradition, which can remain the same. What is important is that it is chosen with the correct intention and feels good and sacred to you.

**Select Your Stones**

You may have already cleansed them and amplified their energy on an altar. Or you may have them held safely in a small pouch. Or you can sit quietly and meditate while you charge them with your energy or the messages channeled from your angels and guides. You may even prefer your client choose the stones they feel are energetically matched to them. Whatever the reason, make it part of your ritual because this will inspire confidence and, practically speaking, make it easier to remember.

**Cast Your Stones**

There are several different ways to cast your stones, and we will talk much more on this, but for the ease of creating practical steps, remember to hold your stones in a pouch or your or your client's hands 2-3 inches above your casting area. Gently pour or cast the stones in the lithomancy space.

**Create the Reading**

Watch where your stones land. Some may roll out of your reading zone, and some may fall to the floor. Wherever they go, decide if you want to omit these stones from your forecast or if their distance from the casting area plays a significant part in your interpretation. What could this mean? Practitioners are divided on this subject, so take some time to think about what it means to you. Which lithomancy tradition or practice are you most aligned with? Again, practice the art, and the answer will be revealed to you in your divine guidance.

**Write Down Your Interpretation**

Remember to record your interpretations. Some of us need time to interpret downloads and divine messages. My spiritual art practice involves sleeping and dreaming about my wisdom, so I can fully understand its meaning. But in the meantime, you should record all the interpretations and meanings you've deciphered for analysis later. Keep a special book or journal to record all findings. You can use a computer to share client information too. You may also have regular clients who need to refer to their previous sessions for clarity.

**Cleanse Your Stones**

Previously, we've talked about cleansing your stones. Choose from sage, moonlight, water, or spiritual cleansing. And make sure that you have a fast method of cleansing you can use in between readings.

**Create a Case Study**

Now, a good lithomancy shaman will create a case study for each client, including themselves, after each reading. This allows you to review your client's readings and go deeper with their questions over time. It also increases your mastery of sacred art and helps to solidify your reputation as a divine lithomancer.

You can adapt these principles to make your lithomancy practice unique to you and your spiritual gifts. Feel free to make changes and have an individual style. That will set you apart from other practitioners in your spiritual field and help shape your brand of lithomancy.

## Distance Dialogues: Interpreting Stone Spreads

The meaning you give to the stones and crystals used in lithomancy will differ from one shaman to the next, and that's perfectly plausible. So, it's crucial to discern how your stones land and their interpretation will depend heavily on the meaning you give to each mineral. However, there are a few ways in which the stones land that can show us patterns or lead us to some theories:

- Usually, lithomancy stones are cast inside a circle like a clock.
- The inside of the clock acts as the next 3 months. The interior is broken up into twelve sections, just like a clock, but these sections represent twelve weeks.
- The outside perimeter of the clock represents a long period.

So, let's take a quick look at the sixteen stones in lithomancy to help us understand the stone arrangement. Ten of the sixteen stones represent the astrological interpretation of the planets, and these are:

1. Sun
2. Moon
3. Mercury
4. Mars
5. Venus
6. Jupiter
7. Saturn
8. Uranus
9. Neptune
10. Pluto

There are also six stones relating to the interests of the client:

1. Love
2. Luck
3. Life
4. Magic
5. Commitment
6. Place

You can also add any other stones with a specific purpose or to help you with a unique question.

Then, using the circle, similar to a clock, you can begin reading the stones, starting at 12 and finishing at 12. Interpret what you see. This lithomancy method is super versatile and highly dependent on your intuitive skills. The significant role and meaning you give to the stones will give you the correct interpretation of your reading.

Firstly, intuition plays the biggest part in interpreting your reading. This is going to help you with the context of your casted stones. This skill must be practiced and will develop over time. You can't hurry this one, so practice, practice, practice!

Secondly, can you see any clusters, patterns, or shapes between the stones? What does that tell you? Please pay special attention to geometric shapes, as they are common indicators (they can be studied further in spiritualism as they have significant importance). A pattern is going to highlight an area of your client's life. Where did the stones fall about that?

Thirdly, stones have different shapes, and some angles on your minerals will act as directors or pointers. Where do the stones point? What does the direction indicate?

Fourthly, are any stones isolated, or did they roll far away or off your table? Have a theory beforehand of the significance of this, so you can see a pattern quickly when it arises.

Lastly, the distance or proximity to other stones will indicate whether these characters work together in harmony or are at odds. Remember the unique quality of each stone and what it can represent to help you decipher the meaning.

Use this guideline to formulate and discover your unique style of stone divination. Again, this sacred art has no right or wrong, only your unique understanding of a stone-casting layout.

## Intuition: The Silent Stone Speaker

Ways to enhance your intuition come from various sources. Still, first, we will touch on the meaning of healing to activate your spiritual gifts. Every human being on this planet can activate their spiritual gift. However, not everyone believes that's true, and while others do believe, they find it impossible to do.

The process of activating spiritual intuition and ability, in theory, is relatively easy. However, as it is predominantly an emotional journey, it presents problems many of us find impossible to face. Humans tend to avoid pain in any way possible, sometimes pulling us away from our spiritual selves.

During the journey of life and in the process of being, we lose parts of ourselves, making us feel incomplete. Usually, losing a part of yourself comes from a difficult or abusive childhood, poor life choices and decision-making, and a lack of education about healing. In dealing with stress and trauma, we close off parts of our emotions and ability to face and cope with pain. Over time, these pieces of our character or personality become lost or blocked, and emptiness fills that void. The more parts of ourselves we lose, the further we drift away from our spiritual selves. This is why the connection to the self is so important. It is the root of your spiritual gift and ability. It can only be tapped into when you accept that healing must occur and you must face things you have buried away, categorized, or blocked off. Your abilities will activate again while accepting and moving through this healing transition. They don't just suddenly appear; you were born with them, and they were always present, but inadvertently you switched them off.

If you cannot access these parts of yourself again, it's a good idea to talk to a spiritual mentor or coach to get help. Often, they can use their psychic guidance to steer you to the parts of healing that would benefit you. And that also makes you feel less alone in an emotional journey.

Secondly, chakra clearing and rebalancing are very beneficial to enhance your intuition. Again, working with a spiritual mentor can be the fastest way to clear blockages and help you realign your energy centers, allowing them access to see what and where the problems lie. You can also do this yourself with a color chart and by simply visualizing the appropriate color around your chakra, meditating, and calling that color in to enhance the centers of your spiritual energy.

You can also use crystals to work in this area too. Crystals are often linked closely with chakras. For example, amethyst is wonderful for opening up the third eye chakra and enabling your spiritual sight. Hold and meditate with your crystal as it radiates and amplifies the energy you need to activate each chakra. This is a beautiful transformational way to call in intuition, and you can do it regularly. It will also give you a much deeper connection with the stones themselves.

Writing or journaling is also a fast way to increase intuition. As we pass the day, our thoughts block our minds and clog them from thinking and feeling clearly. So often, we can become overwhelmed or pulled away from consciousness because of the racing, intrusive, negative, or egotistical thoughts flying through our minds. The biggest battle in life is one with ourselves, mainly from not controlling our minds. An uncontrolled mind is a destructive weapon, but luckily there are many ways to make it work for you instead of against you. Writing down the contents of your head daily frees up space to think clearly and allows intuition to pour in. Get a notebook or journal and answer five daily questions:

1. What was great about today?
2. What could've been better?
3. What did I learn?
4. What do I acknowledge myself for?
5. What are three things I am grateful for?

At the end of the day, spending no more than fifteen minutes a reflection will help you think more clearly and activate parts of yourself that you previously couldn't access. If morning is a better time for you, write then and start your day with a good and focused intention.

If writing is not for you, you could voice record your journal. This allows for the same release method, brain-dumping all that divine information, allowing your mind to be clearer, freer, and ready to accept greater intuition. This process is slow and steady, but it is impactful and progressive!

Thirdly, movement. How does movement increase intuition? Well, this is an interesting topic. You detach yourself from your mind while moving your body in sport, dance, or any way that allows your entire body to move. Now this doesn't always happen immediately, especially if you follow the rules of a game or sport, but take dancing, for example. Focusing on moving different parts of your body speedily forces you to become detached from your thoughts. You feel into the music, the beat, and your body. You open a portal to receive information and begin feeling instead of thinking. Movement is hugely popular, and you can see this every day by watching the number of people that get up in the morning and work out, go to the gym, or run. It's not just to get a great-looking body and stay physically healthy. It creates a neutral and enlightened space to create from in your mind and is a hugely underrated way to release stress and bring in intuitive gifts.

**Meditation**

We've just discussed movement as a means of meditation, but there are also more traditional ways. Meditation is a vast topic, and traditional methods are useful and straightforward. You can easily find a guided meditation on YouTube, sink back with your headphones on, and relax into one. Feel your intention beforehand, guiding your mind into what you want to achieve. After your meditation, you can ask a question such as what do I need to do to increase my intuition today? Usually, you will get an answer that will help you progress along this journey.

Another amazing way to meditate is to get out in nature. Walk barefoot in green areas, free from electromagnetic waves, other people's energy, and the concrete that blocks our spiritual self. The peace and tranquility of nature help us open up and calm down, creating a channel for good thoughts and increased awareness.

Many intuitive psychics are asked how they increase their intuition and psychic ability. One answer came back—how do you get good at math? You practice. And that made me smile because it's correct. Intuition is not reserved for special people and gifted souls. It's inside everyone and is just bobbing up and down under the surface of your skin. Many societal pressures, family, trauma, and poor decisions can alter this. Connecting back to yourself remains the primary source for activating this channel to connect, run, and flow freely.

Now you have the foundation for reading your stones, let's get you into a celestial space to connect with these energetical beings!

## Chapter 7

# Harmonizing with the Hard

Connecting with stones isn't reserved for sacred spiritualists. Still, it is tied to those who want to feel a tangible connection to Mother Gaia. Holding a piece of the glaringly beautiful rock and feeling the vibration within it has transcended the ages and cut across cultures and countries. We even connect to those rocks such as moldavite, which are from far beyond the reaches of our earthly soil.

We adorn them in this fast-paced world but never have crystals, gemstones, rocks, or minerals gone out of fashion. In fact, as time increases, so does their value. With the persistence of those that practice spiritual rituals, life has been breathed back into the stones that once played a significant role in daily living. It's no wonder that our connection to stones is sacred, organic, natural, and ultimately divine.

### Bonding Bridges: Techniques of Togetherness

Some channels and tools connect our higher self to the spiritual realm, and in stone divination, bonding with your stones will be a magical experience. Especially if it's something, you've never tried before. We've already talked about how important it is to choose your stones with your eyes closed, using your intuition to feel the frequency and vibration you are drawn to. Remember, choosing a stone may be quite different by sight. You may be drawn to the bright green, swirling crystal malachite, but you may not want the faery energy of mischievous elves closely linked with this stone from deep in the earth!

Using your intuition in stone divination comes from the very beginning of your practice. And I'm so glad you are here because what you learn from this tiny book will help you get streets ahead of those reading a few articles online and playing a guessing game.

**Journaling**

You're probably feeling slightly confused about your stones right now. After all, there are around sixteen of them, and I know you're getting them mixed up and confused about which one does what! And this is where the simplicity of journaling sweeps in. Keep a record of your stone journey. Detail all your little things, feelings, and intuitive guesses about your stones daily. Use your journal as a diary to expedite your mastery of divination. You won't be sorry! We can't possibly remember and retain all the information we need when starting in lithomancy. Make this a tool you can refer to that will ultimately teach you all you need to know.

**Moonlight Cleansing**

Bonding under the moonlight, what a blissful image of your stones basking in the glorious pearly gray-white while you sit and talk to them, nestled under the stars. Cleansing is another way to boost your connection with your mineral, and as cleansing is imperative, why not make it a labor of love? It would help if you freed your crystals regularly from the vibrations they store from readings and the different clients you'll work with. It is super important that the base frequency of the stone is restored to a neutral level, as they will also vibrate, extract, and emit vibrations from your frequency. This is a truly ritualistic, heavenly way to bond.

**Wearing as Jewelry or Carrying**

Oooh, the easiest way to bond and connect is by wearing your stones in a stone or crystal holder as a pendant or bracelet or simply placing them in your pocket. You can also carry them in your handbag too. The more you wear and have your stones, the more attachment you will feel, and the more messages you will download. And they are pretty darn cute too!

**Meditation and Intention Setting**

Meditation and intention setting with your stones is an incredible way to connect and bond, evoking deep intuition and linking yourself to the divine guidance of the stone's frequency. We'll talk about this in much more detail next. Still, if you can include your stone in daily meditation practice, you're fast-tracking your connection with your crystals. When setting an intention with your stone, ask it a question. Ask your celestial mineral what it is here to tell you. What kind of divine guidance will it bring? And wait for the answer. Do not rush trying to figure things out. The answer will come at the right time. Be patient and open to listening and learning the response from various sources. Now more on meditation and visualization practices.

## MINDSTONE MEDITATIONS

When we meditate, we are less concerned with thoughts and words coming from the mind and become more in tune with our intuition and consciousness. Our ego retracts, and we can think and feel the wisdom of our higher self. This means we process feelings and wisdom from our heart chakra, which aligns with our higher intelligence and intentions. This is fundamental to receiving divine inspiration, celestial guidance, messages from sources, and downloads from our most authentic selves.

During meditation, try and visualize yourself in your divination practice. How do you see yourself in your divination practice? What does it look like to you? How do the stones talk to you? What do you hear? Using these visual aids, you can shape and create your bespoke world of lithomancy. Meditation acts as a key to unlocking your higher guidance. If you tap into it regularly, you will obtain mastery of stone divination much faster than if you don't.

Meditation can take many forms. You don't have to sit cross-legged in silence. This is where many people fail and stop enjoying meditation. You don't need silence to listen, but you do need to be able to disconnect. Get out in nature and ground yourself to the earth with bare feet. Ask the trees and wildlife what you need to learn. Movement is another way to meditate, run, dance, or do something that disconnects you from thoughts and words traveling through your mind. This is where you reach higher states of consciousness. This is where you get knowledge and ideas that make you feel truly fulfilled. Or, as an alternative, you can pray. Praying or similar rituals with a deep connection to sources is beautifully peaceful and magic to reach your higher power.

During any meditation practice, you can incorporate chakra alignment too. Chakras, in their most basic representation, can be recognized with color. If you think, wear, or surround yourself with the color of the chakra, you want to meditate with or use the color of your stone to align the stone frequency with your chakra. This will deepen your connection and integration, both physically and spiritually.

## Close Encounters of the Stone Kind

Looking back on history, we began wearing stone amulets and gemstones around 1600 BC. In a nutshell, stones have been essential to us as jewelry for almost four thousand years. That is a big deal! And this is a perfect way to keep stones close to us, not just because they are jaw-droppingly gorgeous, but because of the depth of connection they create. Now wearing your lithomancy stones as jewelry is only possible if you can return it to a pocket stone after wearing it. But it can be placed in a pendant or bracelet holder and then worn as either accessory. This is highly recommended to bond your stones to your frequency and boost your confidence when casting your stones in a reading.

Pocket stones can be carried anywhere too. Please place them in your handbag so they stay close to your vibration. They will protect you and enhance your vibration, making them perfect travel companions.

Stone energy helps us become resilient and feel protected or grounded. They enhance our power and boost confidence. Stones are a reminder of our intentions, and they help us to pray. They align our energy and amplify it at the same time. Our stones become a powerful part of us, vital to the success of our stone divination reading.

Now we've come so far with your stone divination knowledge, let's look at typical stone layouts and put all this theory into practice. Got your stones ready?

## Chapter 8

# Layouts: The Lithomancy Lexicon

Unconscious, scientific, and modern learning methods will probably make up a considerable part of your knowledge, wisdom, and education at this point in your life. But have you ever wondered why you are drawn to learn about lithomancy and the spiritual rituals and practices that are so enticing? Why are you so fascinated with the magical, mysterious arts that others are not? In fact, why are you so intrigued when others are equally repelled by spiritualism?

Take this as a sign that you have opened your mind and accepted the teaching of the source at a higher level. You've already tapped into your higher self, perhaps unable to access it on demand yet, but you're certainly on your way. Stone divination helps us increase the use of our pineal gland and third eye to access our spiritual gifts and help others in their journey. This is not something new to us as humans. And as we've touched on before, history and varied cultures have dipped their toes in the spiritual pool over the centuries.

While we don't have hard archaeological evidence of stone layouts, we do have handed down practices that we can refer to and support us in our intuitive findings. Again, lithomancy has no right or wrong, only what your intuition speaks and guides.

Please think of the stone layouts we will discuss as a framework for your castings, and never fear the divine information you are about to receive in any form. Let's dive in!

## Time-tested Tablets: Traditional Layouts

There are many different stone layouts in lithomancy, and by now, you may also feel that the types of designs you have read about are confusing and lack detail. And while this may have stirred up some confusion in you, it's significant evidence to show you how personal and different each lithomancy practice is. It also gives you the confidence to know that you can make your lithomancy style of casting unique and bespoke to your system of foretelling the future. Remember, our historical evidence and artifacts from lithomancy relate to the stones that were used. We have to rely on traditions handed down and interpreted, combined with our intuition, to create a format to cast the stones.

Let's look at some of the varied approaches to casting stones.

**Circle Formation**

We can see that the most explained way to cast stone in lithomancy is by using a piece of leather, string, or cloth in a circular shape to throw our stones above and see where they land, inside and outside this circle.

The circle shape can represent a clock, with each number of the clock from one to twelve representing one week. In this way, you can cast your lithomancy stones to read the future of the next three months. The outside of the circle reflects a more extended period. Still, your intuition will tell you how to determine the periods you refer to in your readings.

This is the most common stone layout used in lithomancy as it helps you to draw an accurate reading in a 3-month cycle, week by week. It's simple to use for newcomers to lithomancy. At the same time, you learn how to increase and develop your intuition and psychic abilities.

**The Board Blueprint**

## Divination with Stones

Many different types of boards or charts are referred to by lithomancy practitioners are boards such as Ouija, Feng Shui Bagua boards, astrological charts, or even a chart made up of areas of life that most people want to investigate, namely health, wealth, and relationships, and spirituality. Divine inspiration, downloads, or channeling the stones will allow you to decipher the best way to interpret the board. Always start with a simple, repeatable process that will enable you to remember and repeat it easily until you've mastered the art.

Stone layouts are as varied and different as each lithomancy practitioner. Still, this guide recommends initially focusing on the circle layout for simpler, faster divination mastery.

## The Unfolding of Unique Layouts

So, you now have your structured format or perimeter for casting your stones. You can do this on top of a cloth or mat, and your perimeter can be set out with string or leather. So, let's begin to take the time to understand and interpret the placement of the stones once you have cast them.

Each reading will be different depending on your environment. If you have personal clients, you can ask them to hold and drop the stones themselves over the casting board or circle. Alternatively, if the casting is done over the phone or via video link, you can ask your client to say "drop" when they feel the moment is right. Either way holds the same power; you can use the method you feel comfortable with. This is your lithomancy practice, after all.

If we use the clock formation as the most straightforward guide to help us read the casting, apply the following conditions:

- Each hour of the clock represents one week in a 3-month cycle.
- The circle's interior represents the next 3 months, and the exterior represents a different time. Does the

exterior of the circle mean these stones are not included in the reading, or does this refer to a time outside the 3-month framework? Does this area outside have any bearing on your client's immediate query? Or does this refer to the past, present, or future?
- Identify any patterns or clusters between the stones—does this reflect chaos or harmony?
- Look at how the stones are pointed. If you have already decided that if your stone points up or down, left or right, that has a significant meaning, how does this affect the details of your reading? Consider deciding these things before casting and refer to how you use a pendulum when determining what movement is yes and which means no.
- Read your casting clockwise, in the same way you would a clock.
- Patterns of stones may refer to something symbolic in your readings. The more you practice your casting, the easier you can see.
- The circle's center represents your client's immediate thoughts and concerns; after reading this, you can work clockwise around the circle.
- If two or three stones are touching or on each other, what does that represent? Knowing the precise meanings of your stones will guide you here.
- Decide where your stones are pointing. In lithomancy, pointing north is generally towards the future, and pointing south reflects the past.
- If the stones are close together, this represents a time that will pass quickly. If the stones are a long way apart, those reflect a slow pace of time.
- Identify the shapes and patterns of the stones that land together. A circle may represent harmony and

flow. Stones pointing away from each other may not reflect flow or changing times.

Ultimately, focus on the meaning of the stones and how they point.

## Custom Creations: Your Layout Legacy

Developing your stone layout will be unique and bespoke to your divine stone divination practice. And this is the part where you can be super creative and pour love and spice into your lithomancy sacred art. What does lithomancy mean to you? Which culture or tradition resonates the most with you, or do you have ancestral ties to a particular practice? Are you a crystal fanatic and already know and love the stones? You just haven't put them to work yet? There are so many questions you can ask yourself. Still, ultimately, it's about what looks right, feels right, and is simple for you to understand and develop. Because that's precisely what you will do from here!

**Select Your Stones**

This has to be the most fun part of setting up your stone divination. Now you can select any stone that has significance to you. Don't be swayed by any practitioner, witch, or warlock! You have to information you need to create a stunning and high-frequency lithomancy casting set. Choose wisely because stones and crystals will work when you pick the right ones aligned and connected to you!

**Give Meanings to Your Stones**

The stones you choose and their meanings are designed by you. Stone frequencies vibrate with people on many different levels. What do your stones represent? What do they try and tell you? Choose and apply meanings to them and see how they respond. You can develop these meanings over time too.

**Decide a Stone Layout**

The determining factor of choosing a stone layout is where

you will operate your divination practice. Do you want to make it simple and something you can take anywhere? Or do you want a fixed location with a cleansing area and altar? Take some time to negotiate your thoughts and decide what's best for you. You can always change and develop your location as you grow. Maybe you want to have both options. Remember, this is your divine practice. You get to choose how it looks and operates.

**Conducting a Reading**

This is the first time we have discussed managing clients and the practical aspects of dealing with enquirers. How many questions will you allow your client to ask? How long will your appointment time be? Research shows that thirty minutes to an hour is the expected reading time. Will you allow lots of questioning back and forth or up to three questions in one reading?

**Niche Readings**

Do you offer a niche in your lithomancy practice? Do you want to be known for love and relationship readings, or will you cover other aspects of life? What resonates with you, and what is easy for your intuition to pick up? Many experts can become well-known for focusing on one area.

**Alignment**

Your stone divination practice should be aligned with you. It would help if you made it feel, reflect, and shine like you. You will attract those that feel into this alignment and vibration.

Now you have all the ingredients to make a start in lithomancy. How does it feel to enter the world of stone divination? Exciting, confusing, scary? In reality, it will be a mixture of all of those, and that's completely normal. We all start at the beginning as beginners! Take some time now to set up your practice. Take your time and dilute all the divine findings you've learned. Then come back and get started on advancing your techniques in stone divination.

## Chapter 9

# Mastering the Mystic Mineral

There are no specific advanced techniques to call upon in stone divination. These are the only ways to enhance and boost your lithomancy practice. Once you acquire more knowledge, you expand your sacred foretelling art and take it into more significant realms of practice. Make sure that you are fully competent in the basic structure of lithomancy first before trying to cast your net wider. Deep then wide is always the best recipe for expansion and advancement!

## Divination Duo: Lithomancy and Beyond

The big question is, can lithomancy be combined with other methods of divination? Well, the answer is yes, of course! Because divine download or inspiration comes directly from the source, any methods of foretelling the future can be combined with lithomancy. Remember, your intuition will guide you on this journey. As you explore the spiritual realm of gifts, abilities, and historical data, you'll see a new world of methods and practices that will call to you.

**Crystal Clear: Crystallomancy**

Let's look at Lithomancy's closest partner, crystallomancy.

Now even the exact framework of crystallomancy is open to interpretation. In this sacred practice, crystals have specific interpreted meanings the practitioner can draw on to enhance a lithomancy reading. Crystallomancy gives specific meaning to its stones, as detailed by the healer, Judy Hall:

- Agate: Worldly success, a journey
- Black Agate: Courage and prosperity
- Red Agate: Health and longevity
- Amber: A voyage
- Amethyst: Life changes and shifts in consciousness
- Aquamarine: New friends
- Aventurine: Growth and expansion
- Bloodstone: Distressing news is on the way
- Blue Lace Agate: Healing is needed
- Cats Eye: Beware of treachery
- Chalcedony: Friends reunited
- Chrysoberyl: A time of need
- Chrysolite: Exercise caution
- Coral: Recovery from illness
- Diamond/Quartz: Permanence, love, victory over enemies
- Emerald/Peridot: Much to look forward to
- Garnet: The solution to a mystery
- Hematite: New opportunities
- Jade: Immortality and perfection
- Jasper: Earthly affairs are successful Love returned
- Lapis Lazuli: Divine favor
- Milky/Snow Quartz: Profound changes occur
- Moonstone: Watch out for self-deception or illusions
- Moss Agate: An unsuccessful journey
- Onyx: A happy marriage
- Opal: Great possessions
- Quartz: Clarify issues, speak out
- Rose Quartz: Love and self-healing

- Ruby/Garnet: Power and passion, unexpected guests
- Sapphire: Truth and chastity, escape from danger
- Snowflake Obsidian: End of challenging time
- Tigers Eye: All is not as it seems
- Topaz: No harm shall befall
- Tourmaline: An accident
- Turquoise: Prosperity, new job
- Unakite: Compromise and integration are needed

And to give a more direct reading, crystallomancy has gemstones for days of the week:

- Sunday: Ruby
- Monday: Moonstone
- Tuesday: Coral
- Wednesday: Emerald
- Thursday: Cat's eye
- Friday: Diamond (quartz)
- Saturday: Sapphire

## And Months of the Year:

- January: Garnet
- February: Amethyst
- March: Bloodstone
- April: Diamond (quartz)
- May: Emerald
- June: Agate
- July: Carnelian
- August: Sardonyx
- September: Sapphire
- October: Aquamarine
- November: Topaz
- December: Turquoise

**Even Countries of the World and US States:**

- Agate: Kentucky, Maryland, Louisiana, Minnesota, Montana, Nebraska, New York, South Dakota, Tennessee, Oregon, Denmark and Panama
- Ajoite: South Africa and Arkansas
- Amber: France, Sicily and Romania
- Amethyst: South Carolina and Uruguay
- Aragonite: Spain
- Beryl: New Hampshire
- Carnelian: Norway and Sweden
- Celestite: Pennsylvania
- Danburite: Connecticut
- Diamond: South Africa, England and the Netherlands
- Emerald: North Carolina, Peru and Spain
- Flint: Ohio
- Garnet: Czechia and Alaska
- Almandine Garnet: Connecticut
- Star Garnet: Idaho
- Grossular Garnet: Vermont
- Granite: New Hampshire, North and South Carolina, Wisconsin and Vermont
- Hematite: Alabama
- Herkimer Diamond: Herkimer County, USA
- Jade: New Zealand, China, Turkestan, Alaska and Wyoming
- Labradorite: Oregon
- Lapis Lazuli: Egypt, Bolivia, Chile and Bokhara
- Moonstone: Florida
- Turquoise: Arizona, New Mexico, Nevada, Turkey and Iran
- Tourmaline: Maine, New England and Brazil
- Topaz Blue: Topaz is a Texas state stone and Utah's yellow

## Divination with Stones

- Sunstone: Oregon
- Smoky Quartz: New Hampshire and Scotland
- Serpentine: California and Rhode Island
- Sapphire: Montana, United States
- Ruby: Thailand and Myanmar
- Rose Quartz: South Dakota and South Africa
- Rhodonite: Massachusetts and Russia
- Rhodochrosite: Colorado and Peru
- Quartz: Arkansas, Iowa, Georgia and Switzerland
- Petrified Wood: Alberta, Mississippi and Washington
- Peridot: Hawaii and Egypt
- Opal: Nevada, New South Wales and Hungary
- Obsidian: Mexico
- Morganite (Pink Beryl): Madagascar

This method can be combined with your lithomancy board or perimeter to give an in-depth reading. Still, it's important to note that there is much more to remember in this practice. It would help to provide more time to learn your stones so you don't misinterpret your casting messages. This divination practice also requires you to have an extensive range of crystals. So definitely something to consider when you have mastered the techniques of lithomancy first and a fun way of developing your psychic skills.

**Sight of the Scrying**

Scrying or crystal ball reading is another form of divination that compliments lithomancy. Sitting with your crystals in a deep meditation or trance-like state, you can ask your crystal or ball questions, wait for divine messages, or look into the crystal ball to see a vision. These are not complicated ways of using your psychic abilities, but they require you to tap into your intuition and higher self easily and swiftly, especially when working with clients.

**Pendulum Prophesies**

Another fun way of developing and combining divination methods with lithomancy is using a pendulum. Ensure you've programmed your pendulum by knowing which movement represents yes and which swing represents no. Then, once your stone casting reading is in action, use your pendulum to go deeper into any questions your client may have, giving a more detailed response and depth to your reading.

**Tarot Trails**

Tarot cards can also be used alongside lithomancy. However, working with tarot requires much additional knowledge and understanding and the ability to open and close portals. While this is a fun way to develop your practice, more care must be taken alongside more learning to make it effective and safe.

## Rituals: The Stone Ceremonies

There are three prominent rituals that most divine healers use, and the stones from our divination practice can be beautifully incorporated here. Dive deep into these rituals with your stones to enhance your connection with them and boost confidence in your intuition and lithomancy practice.

**Moonstone Magic**

This is a magical time to feel all the force and flow of the mysterious, feminine moon. Bathe your stones in the moonlight for at least three hours. Moonlight not only cleanses your stones but helps to charge them too. The stones build strength under the pearlish-gray light of the moon. Toxins and negative frequencies are drawn out and neutralized, and your stones are ready to recharge or program. Their base frequency realigns and gets supercharged under the milky night sky. A simple ritual can be created with your stones, and repeating this under every full moon will see your intuition explode with possibility, and your spiritual gifts strengthen organically.

**Crystal Grid Gala**

Crystal grids are an incredible way of calling in power to your lithomancy work. Crystal grids start with an intention, motivation, or idea. What do you want your crystal grid to do? Be specific with its program, for example, a crystal grid to keep out unwanted visitors when increasing psychic ability or a grid for deeper learning at exam time. What is your lithomancy practice lacking right now? Make a crystal grid and incorporate your stones to make them more powerful and burst with energy. Crystal grids are very popular, and you can easily access more information on the best crystals.

**Blessing of the Boulders**

Like the stone blessing rituals in many pagan wedding ceremonies, you can create a ritual to bless your lithomancy divination stones. Just like you would hold a wedding stone for the engaged couple during the wedding ceremony, blessing it throughout the nuptial rite, you can hold your rocks and minerals, saying a prayer or downloading an intention to be divinely received by the stone. And you can activate this ritual at pertinent times of the year, like the summer or winter solstice, depending on what culture or tradition you are attuned with.

## Deepening the Dialogue

Deepening a spiritual practice is a journey with no destination. Along this journey, a lot will change; you will develop your spiritual gifts, you will heal, your mind will expand, your compassion will grow, and your life will unfold as you begin to attract what is truly yours.

**Here are the top 5 ways to deepen your lithomancy practice:**

**Mediate Regularly**

Bring stillness and awareness to your mind. Set intentions and see how they process and grow your lithomancy practice. Meditating and calling in your higher power is the one thing that will become your driving force and your tap to increased knowledge.

**Begin the Healing Journey**

This has to be the most significant part of deepening your lithomancy practice or any spiritual practice. In experiencing trauma, we block off, classify, and resist parts of ourselves to avoid pain. A perfectly natural human response. But in doing so, you lose parts of yourself, reducing your capacity as a human and celestial being. You get pushed off your path of alignment and life purpose. Starting the healing process is like solving a puzzle, retrieving the lost pieces, and putting them back together. And during this process, your spiritual gifts will expand and grow along with your divination practice as you become enlightened and back to who you have always been before exterior circumstances affected you.

**Pray**

Praying is a way of setting your intention and seeking gratitude. Gratitude will fill your heart and make you receptive to receiving more. This will spill over into your divination work and fill up your lithomancy practice. Your readings will become more meaning full and more seraphic.

**Move Your Body**

Movement gives us organic detachment from the thoughts and feelings of our mind. It helps us to detach our body and feel rather than think, boosting our intuitive skills. The perfect way to meditate and set intentions.

**Read and Learn About Spirituality**

Ultimately, we need the knowledge and wisdom of others to increase ours. Always read more about historical and new spiritual practices. Get ideas from others and make them your own. Learn from spiritual mentors and coaches that can push you to become a better version of yourself.

Deeping your lithomancy through these spiritual ways won't come quickly, and don't expect to be able to incorporate them all at once. We all have normal, busy, working lives, but if you can find a way to include one practice into your day, your streets are ahead of everybody else.

And now that you're there let's see how other real-life applications of stone divination have helped others.

## Chapter 10

## The Ethical Edifice

When you start to exchange money for services, a new world opens up, which will not only turn you into a divination master but a businesswoman too. And suppose you want to be taken seriously and make your passion for the sacred art of stone divination a business to grow and flourish. In that case, this next chapter will be very useful for you!

### The Resolute Reader: Responsible Rites

**Ethical Code of Conduct**

When working with clients, particularly in the spiritual field, it's important to adhere to an ethical code of conduct. To have a clear set of guidelines to work to. Working and discussing sensitive issues requires a good level of confidentiality and clarity. Your clients to know what they can expect from a reading and also that the content of your conversation and file will be kept confidential.

**Manage Your Client's Expectations, Too**

Don't promise the world. Be clear on how many questions they can ask and appointment duration for the reading. Very often, clients can be disappointed because they misunderstood something. Remember, you are not promising results but guidance and clarity on a certain matter or timeframe.

Have a privacy policy so clients know their details will be kept safe and not sold to other companies.

**Be Professional**

Have a code of standards and treat your customers equally. Word soon spreads if you give more to one client than another when they pay the same price. Be mindful when giving discounts or reduced prices. Clients can feel upset if they are not paying the same price. It's always better to reward clients in a different way than to cut prices.

**Client-Centered Business**

Make sure your clients are at the center of your business. After all, this may be your business, but everything is about your client. Without them, you have no business. This means building long-term relationships with clients for repeat business and referrals. To do this, your clients must be at the center of your business.

Continuous professional development: You may have already heard of CPD for continuous professional development. This shows your commitment to your trade and confirms to your client that you take your profession seriously. It's good to update your skills at least once a year in some learning space or professional setting.

Consent: In our modern day, it's beneficial to get your client to sign a consent form, especially in the health and well-being field, which spirituality services spill into. Refunds and complaints can quickly be resolved with the right documentation. This doesn't have to cost you a fortune. Still, if you have a legitimate business, you need the correct documentation to avoid problems in the future.

Respecting your stones: Last but by no means least, respect your stones. They are pivotal to the success of your practice. Have an altar of sacred space where they can charge and keep their energetic alignment. Your clients will see this as a good sign of professionalism, building trust.

## Privacy and Pebbles: Ethical Engagement

**Data Protection:** When dealing with clients and payments, having a data protection policy in place is professional. It shows you are a legitimate business and you take working protocol seriously. It also helps to build trust with your client. It reflects professionalism while making your practice secure and free from misunderstandings, accusations, or fraud.

**Confidentiality:** Handling your client's details is one thing, but ensuring complete confidentiality for your client is another. You may get super exciting results in your readings, but these are not necessarily your results to share. When we overshare personal details, not only does it destroy trust, but it opens the door to fraudulent activity. Trust forms the basis of any good relationship, including business.

**Posting in Social Media:** So many of our clients now come from social media. We build an audience, create content, and post it online. We mustn't overshare client details, even if you have excellent results. Always ask your client's permission first, and wherever possible, get written consent.

**Emotions:** By this point, you are probably already aware that foretelling, looking into the past, and dealing with matters that worry a sensitive soul will bring about heightened emotions. What do you do in those situations, and how can you make your client feel protected? Firstly, your client details are confidential and should never be discussed with others. Because as much as you think this won't happen to you, please love to share information. And oversharing could damage your business and your reputation. But clients also need to feel safe in your care. They may come to you with personal, emotional issues and need support and a listening ear. Under these circumstances, you must not become overwhelmed and learn how to deal sensitively with clients.

## THE STONE SOURCING SAGA

Ensuring ethical sourcing of stones is paramount in your business for many reasons. Let's take a deeper look at some of those now to get your spiritual practice perfectly aligned.

### Sourcing Stones and Their Energy

The energetical transaction of your stones makes up the foundation of your stone divination practice. Stones, crystals, rocks, and minerals are selected because of the vibration they emit, and this creates their value and makes them a reliable source in your castings. So, the energy from the stone is important to you, your business, and your client. You must source your stones from a place that supports ethical working practices. You must ensure that your stones come from an environment where no one gets hurt or is forced to work under terrible conditions. Your stones will be programmed with the energy of their origin. Make sure that origin is free from harm, destruction, and terror.

### Fair-Trade

We see cheap crystals everywhere in the modern world, and many times we question, how is this possible? And I am sure that we turn a blind eye to the answer. Trackable, traceable stones are worth every penny. Not only will they give off amazing frequencies, but your business will be reputable, and this is also where you can charge more for your services. Don't let a poor money mindset creep in and offer low prices because you're or don't think anyone will pay your prices. Ensure the supplier you purchase from is paid relatively to ensure a fair price for your services. The karma wheel is always turning, and what you do will return to you, good or bad.

### Environmental Responsibility

Don't support suppliers destroying Mother Gaia when

purchasing crystals, stones, and minerals. Think about your impact on this world.

**Support Small Businesses**

Working in this fantastic field of metaphysics, you'll have the opportunity to support small businesses across the globe. In the far-flung corners of the earth, you will come across artisan miners and craftsmen that live in unreachable places that can provide you with the most sensational rocks and minerals. Please support these businesses and help them to feed that back, not their culture and local community, nurturing and staying grateful for all the opportunities the earth brings you.

**Traceable Stones and Evidence:**

- Track your mineral inventory.
- Make sure there is a trace back to the source of your rocks and gemstones.
- Ask your supplier for all details of the source and movement of the rock, along with the ethical guidelines for craftsmen or miners.
- Be a reputable, responsible, and caring stone divination practitioner known for your commitment to Mother Gaia, and this will also act as a huge selling point for your business.

Energy and karma are vast aspects of your world now. Remember that, and move through all the dimensions with kindness and love. And in our last chapter, we will see exactly how to do that!

## Chapter 11

# Living the Lithomancy Legacy

You will be instantly recognizable once you embrace stone divination as a lifestyle. Your business will mostly run on referrals, and the power of the stones and spiritual foretelling will be abundant within you.

### Daily Divination: Stones in the Sunlight

**Morning Meditation**

What a beautiful way to begin your day by meditating with your chosen stone. Enlightenment and focus will pour through when you commit to this practice. Your overall health and well-being improve, and divine messaging or downloads will become clear.

**Free Reading for Practice**

Regularly practice your stone readings with family and friends. This will increase your confidence and knowledge and further your connection with your stones. Set up a ritual and time to help those around you, who will help you by being a point of focus in your casting.

**Creating Case Studies and Advertising**

Create case studies and begin recording your findings in your readings. This will enhance trust in your spiritual gifts and allow you to create content if social media is your marketing ground. Talks sensitively about your findings and openly ask others what they experience. This is a great learning tool while stamping your mastery into something tangible.

**Journaling and Reflection**

Journaling or simply writing things down is an excellent way to record your case findings, how you feel, and what you learned. It allows us to reflect and receive valuable insights and experiences. It also helps us to look back when we get stuck to see how we moved on or grew from a sticking point.

**Setting Intentions**

Being entirely focused is where we act and implement those ideas. Setting your daily intention will help you achieve a bigger goal, one step at a time. Use your crystals or stones to help you, and you'll be surprised at the outcome!

**Creating Rituals**

Having a stone ritual will create a habit that will become part of your daily life. Between clients, you must follow a process to cleanse your stones for their correct energetic alignment. But it would help if you also had a ritual for cleansing them against your frequency. This is just one ritual. There are so many more you can create. An especially effective one is to create a process with your client so they are free from intrusive thoughts during your stone casting. This will help the divine message come through easily and intuitively. And if your intuition is lacking, or you are continuously distracted, make sure you have a ritual to develop trust within yourself. This will make you an amazing diviner and an incredible businesswoman too.

## Spirited Stones: The Path of Personal Growth

There are many parts to cultivating your intuition and spiritual growth, which are open to debate. But after many discussions with practitioners and spiritual mentors, these are the most effective ways to grow your spiritual gifts and Faith.

**Healing: The Heart of the Hard**

As we've mentioned several times in this book, spiritual growth is a journey without a destination. There is unlimited access to the spiritual realm and its gifts and blessings never end. They develop and evolve. And if you want the fast-track version of this journey, it's time to look inside yourself and see what needs to be healed. The more blocks and resentment, resistance, and negativity we carry, the more we remain far away from the most authentic version of ourselves. And these things can be released. Not cut away from us because these experiences are invaluable to our understanding, no matter how hard. Sometimes we may even need to repeat these traumatic lessons if we do not master the learning! This is a process, and it can be a painful process but a freeing journey back to us, our highest version, and the one that lives in their life's purpose. You'll see abundance and life's riches unfolding upon making decisions from your heart, space, and soul. And, of course, activation and growth of your intuition and spiritual gifts.

**Self-Study: The Soul of Stone**

One thing that may make you stray from your enlightened path is a need for more learning. There are various ways of increasing your spiritual knowledge without studying if that's not for you. Take part in local events and socialize with your spiritual community. You will learn much more from one person's experience than from one book or YouTube video.

Sign up for a spiritual mentor or coach and participate in a spiritual journey where an expert can help and guide you. Remember to push yourself through those sticking points and places you fear going alone. This will activate you in ways you can't imagine, and the benefits to your world and business will explode.

Take a course and read books. Keep simple study a part of your daily routine to enhance your spiritual gifts. Many psychics say that repetition is the only way to develop a spiritual gift. Follow experts and where others have trail blazed in this sacred space. You will intuitively be drawn to study areas that may not directly relate to stone divination. However, everything you open in your mind will become a tool for deeper intuition or spiritual expansion.

**Community of Crystals: The Social Spectrum**

Joining a local community can be extremely rewarding and beneficial. You may find a practitioner who wants to collaborate and learn from you. Sharing how you operate your gift will be of fascination to others. It will also help you access parts of yourself that you may think are unavailable, as the things that make us feel uncomfortable are always growth opportunities. You'll make some fantastic witchy, wizardry friends, and maybe a peer or ten to help you!

## Reflecting on the Rock: The Lithomancy Lifestyle

Stone defining is a sacred practice open and available to anyone who feels connected to this earth and Mother Gaia. What is beautiful about a stone divining business is that it costs little money to set up. You can work in this business from home, and the space you need to offer your stone readings can be manageable. No huge financial outlay is required, and you can start from where you are now. This is a huge advantage in starting your business without feeling overwhelmed by financial costs. However, there is a small danger that you won't be committed to your practice because you are not investing in yourself financially. But I trust in the power of the stones and know that once you feel the energetical transaction of this sacred art, you will fall in love in a way you can never unlearn. Stones are precious in many ways; we've loved them over the centuries, and that love has never dissipated. It's grown and grown and gets stronger every day. The benefits of stone divination are huge, and it is a practice that helps people discover the good in their life. It helps people achieve their dreams and move away from negative feelings and worries by making positive steps to change their world. Lithomancy in the modern-day world works extremely well by creating a map to live by, giving us a sense of power to know that we are empowering our own decisions with the guidance of our higher self, and our intuition, combined with the guidance from our spiritual realm, ancestors, and guardians. There is simply nothing more beautiful.

You never know where this journey into this lithomancy will take you. You never know how you will impact other people's lives, and very few professions in today's society allow us to do that. What will lithomancy bring to your life? How can you see the effects of stone divination enhancing your world? Is this a doorway to opening more spiritual gifts for yourself? The answers are unknown and endless, but if you follow your intuition and heart, you will find them very soon. Despite what you may read about or hear about spirituality, it's important to trust your intuition when working in a spiritual business. Hopefully, you already feel a connection to stone divination. Perhaps this stems from your culture or your ethnic origin, or maybe you've read about foretelling the future with stones, and this idea seems so exciting to you. Either way, it doesn't matter. Sometimes we are aligned with things we know nothing about in this lifetime, and learning about them is where the excitement stacks up and takes us into the new world of learning progression and growth. Bring this ancient art of foretelling the future into your life. I promise you, you'll never be sorry because stone divination also helps us with how we view time and gives us keys to unlock better decision-making within set time frames.

For some of us, how we think about time allows us to divine or map our future. If we can see into time and space and predict the months that reflect prosperity or find the right time to do something, it helps us take control of our lives.

Beginning your practice in lithomancy will expand your mind into multi-dimensions. You will open, and close portals, and the magic and mystery of life's wonders will start to unfold. You will begin to experience levels; another one will appear every time you reach a new level. This is your spiritual growth. This is your intuition. Getting stronger by the day. Every client you read for will be an opportunity for learning and growth. All the experience you have, both good and bad, will push you towards mastery. Nothing in this journey will be easy, but not worth doing ever is. You're on your path to your life's purpose. You have everything you need to become a lithomancy diviner, and the journey starts here!

## Chapter 12

# Interpreting the Stone Meanings

Interpreting the results of a lithomancy reading is both an art and a science. While the traditional meanings of stones provide a solid foundation, your intuition and personal connection with the stones play a pivotal role in understanding the nuances of a reading.

1. **Types of Stones and Their Meanings**:

   - **Quartz**: Known as the master healer, clear quartz amplifies energy and thought. In a reading, it could signify clarity, amplification of surrounding energies, or the need for purification.
   - **Amethyst**: A spiritual stone, amethyst enhances intuition and spiritual growth. It might suggest a call to deepen one's spiritual practice or the presence of protective energies.
   - **Jasper**: Grounding and stabilizing. Jasper might indicate the need for grounding or highlight areas where stability is required.

Each stone carries its own energy and message. Please familiarize yourself with various stones and their traditional meanings to add depth to your interpretations.

1. **Color Symbolism**:

Colors have symbolic meanings across various cultures. While interpreting stones in a lithomancy reading, consider the color of the stone:

- **Red**: Passion, energy, or a call to action.
- **Blue**: Communication, tranquility, and intuition.
- **Green**: Growth, prosperity, and health.
- **Black**: Protection, mystery, or the unknown.

Always consider how the stone's color complements or contrasts its inherent properties.

1. **Shapes and Patterns**:

The way stones fall and the patterns they create are as important as the stones themselves. For instance:

- **Circular Patterns** Often signify cycles, completion, or the need for holistic thinking.
- **Straight Lines**: Can represent direct action, clarity, or straightforward paths.
- **Scattered Stones**: This might suggest scattered energies or a need to gather oneself and focus.

1. **Personal Resonance and Intuition**:

While traditional meanings and symbolism provide guidelines, personal intuition is paramount. With time, you'll find that certain stones or patterns start resonating in specific ways unique to you. Trust these insights. Remember, the stones serve as a medium. Your intuition, experience, and connection translate their energies into meaningful guidance.

**Crafting a Narrative**

After considering the stones' individual properties, craft a cohesive narrative based on the overall pattern, your intuition, and the question or intention set before the reading. Like pieces of a puzzle, each stone adds to the bigger picture. It's up to the reader to piece these together in a way that resonates with the seeker.

**Trusting Your Intuition in Lithomancy**

Lithomancy, like all forms of divination, is a delicate balance of knowledge and instinct. While the stones hold specific energies and properties that guide interpretations, the reader's intuitive connection and unique journey breathe life into a reading, providing depth, nuance, and specificity.

**Intuition: The Heartbeat of Lithomancy**
**What is Intuition?**

Intuition, often described as a 'gut feeling' or an 'inner voice,' is an innate ability to understand or know something without conscious reasoning. In the context of lithomancy, it's that unspoken pull towards a certain interpretation or the sudden insights that come forth while reading the stones.

**Developing Your Intuitive Abilities**:

Like a muscle, intuition can be strengthened and refined. Meditative practices, journaling, and even paying attention to your gut feelings in everyday situations can help heighten your intuitive senses.

**Trusting Your Intuition**:

For many, trusting their intuition can be challenging, especially when starting out. Remember, lithomancy is as much about the journey as the destination. With practice, trust will naturally build as you witness the accuracy and depth of insights guided by your intuition.

**Personal Experience: The Compass in Your Lithomancy Journey**
**Past Readings as Guideposts**:

Every reading you conduct adds a layer to your understanding and connection with the stones. Over time, patterns might emerge that are unique to your readings. A particular stone always appears for questions about love, or certain patterns recur in times of change. Observing and noting these patterns can provide invaluable insights for future readings.

**Emotional Resonance:**

Personal experiences shape the emotions and energies we bring to a reading. For instance, if you've recently undergone a significant transformation, you might resonate deeply with stones or patterns signifying change. This resonance can guide more nuanced readings for others or even yourself.

**Learning from Feedback:**

If you read for others, their feedback can be an enlightening tool. Over time, you'll begin to see where your strengths lie and where there might be room for growth. This iterative feedback loop and personal reflection can enrich your readings and interpretations significantly.

**Blending Intuition and Experience**

To truly master lithomancy, blending intuition with personal experience is essential. Here's how:

- **Stay Open and Receptive**: Approach each reading with an open heart and mind. While personal experience offers guidance, be receptive to new insights that flow through intuition.
- **Reflect and Journal**: After each reading, spend some time reflecting. What did you feel during the reading? Were there any solid intuitive pulls? How does this reading compare to past ones? Journaling these reflections can offer valuable insights over time.
- **Seek Community**: Engaging with a community of lithomancers can offer fresh perspectives and insights. Sharing experiences and interpretations can help refine your own skills and understanding.

While the stones serve as tangible tools guiding the readings, the ethereal energies of intuition and the wisdom of personal experience truly bring the messages to life. For those embarking on or continuing their lithomancy journey, trust in your inner voice and cherish every experience, for they are the true guides in this mystical art.

**Unraveling the Symbols**

As you embark on the lithomancy journey, recognizing recurring patterns and symbols can significantly aid in interpreting readings. Here are some common themes to look out for:

1. **Clusters and Isolations**:

- **Stone Clusters**: When stones cluster together, it often indicates a concentration of energy or focus in a particular area of the querent's life. Depending on the stones involved, this can suggest strong connections, collaborations, or even potential conflicts.
- **Isolated Stones**: A solitary stone, distanced from the rest, might signify feelings of loneliness, a need for introspection, or a unique path one must tread alone.

1. **Circular Patterns and Straight Lines**:

- **Circular Patterns**: Circles often represent cycles, wholeness, or a need for balance. A stone pattern forming a circle could suggest a phase coming full circle, a balanced approach, or the interconnectedness of certain aspects of one's life.
- **Straight Lines**: These patterns imply directness, clarity, or a straightforward path. If stones form a line, it might point toward a clear direction or suggest a need for direct communication.

1. **Central Stones and Outliers**:

- **Central Stones**: A stone positioned centrally, among others, often plays a significant role in the reading. This could represent the querent themselves, a primary issue at hand, or a pivotal influence in the current situation.
- **Outliers**: Stones on the periphery or outside the main cluster can signify external influences, overlooked aspects, or potential challenges or opportunities from unexpected quarters.

1. **Paths and Barriers**:

- **Stone Paths**: If stones form a pathway, it often indicates a journey or progression. This could be a spiritual journey, a career path, or personal growth. The nature of the stones involved will provide further insights.
- **Barrier Patterns**: When stones form a barrier or wall-like pattern, it may indicate obstacles, blockages, or protective boundaries. Such a pattern calls for reflection on current challenges or understanding one's boundaries.

**Themes Derived from Stone Types**

While patterns provide overarching themes, the nature of the stones involved adds depth:

- **Clear Quartz**: Being the master healer, if this stone dominates a reading, it often signals clarity, healing, or the amplification of surrounding energies.
- **Amethyst**: A stone of spiritual intuition, its prominence might suggest a call for spiritual deepening or protection.

- **Black Obsidian**: Known for grounding and protection, it might hint at the need for grounding or address threats and challenges.

Like a fingerprint, each reading is unique, capturing a moment in time, a question's essence, and the energies surrounding it. Understanding and recognizing the common symbols and themes allows you to dive deeper into the narratives the stones weave, extracting richer insights and guidance.

## Chapter 13

# Creating Your Own Lithomancy Set: A Personal Touch to Divination

Crafting a personalized lithomancy set is more than just a creative endeavor—it's a spiritual journey in and of itself. Here are some profound benefits of personalizing your own collection:

1. **Enhanced Connection**: When you personally select each stone or adorn it with symbols that hold meaning to you, you form a bond with those stones. This bond amplifies the accuracy and depth of your readings.
2. **Unique Energy Signatures**: Every individual has a unique energy signature. By choosing your own stones, they become imbued with your essence, making the divination process smoother and more intuitive.
3. **Empowerment**: Creating your own set empowers you as a diviner. You're not just using a tool—you're using something you've invested time, energy, and intention into.

**Finding or Buying Stones that Resonate with You**

The beauty of lithomancy lies in the infinite possibilities

presented by the stones themselves. The universe is replete with myriad stones, each holding its own vibration and meaning. Here's how to find or buy those that resonate with you:

1. **Intuitive Selection**: Begin by visiting a local crystal or metaphysical shop. Walk around, allowing your intuition to guide you. Sometimes, a stone will call out to you, either by its color, shape, or the energy it exudes.
2. **Research Stone Meanings**: While intuition is paramount, it can also be beneficial to understand the traditional meanings of stones. For instance, rose quartz is often linked with love, while amethyst is known for spiritual growth. Knowing these associations can add layers of depth to your readings.
3. **Natural Settings**: Nature is the best shop for a lithomancer! Rivers, beaches, forests, and mountains are teeming with stones waiting to be discovered. By sourcing your own stones from nature, you imbue your set with raw, unfiltered energy and create a sacred bond with Mother Earth.
4. **Ethical Considerations**: If buying stones, ensure they are ethically sourced. The stone's energy can be tainted if it's procured through harmful means.

**Adding Personal Symbols or Inscriptions to Enhance Connection**

Once you have your stones, the next step is to make them truly yours. Personalizing your stones with symbols or inscriptions makes them unique and amplifies your connection to them.

1. **Selecting Symbols**: Choose symbols that hold personal meaning to you. This could be anything—a rune, a personal sigil, a symbol from your dream, or

even an astrological sign. The key is that it must resonate deeply with you.

2. **Inscription Techniques**: There are several ways to inscribe your stones:

- **Engraving**: This requires special tools and skills. If you're not comfortable doing it yourself, consider hiring a professional.
- **Painting**: Use durable paint or ink, ensuring it's safe for the stone type. Remember, the symbol should last but not harm the stone's natural energy.
- **Temporary Markings**: If you don't want a permanent symbol, consider using biodegradable inks or natural dyes that can be washed off.

1. **Infusing with Intent**: As you inscribe each stone, focus on your intention. Visualize the energy of the symbol merging with the stone, enhancing its divinatory properties.

Creating your own lithomancy set is a journey of introspection, creativity, and spiritual bonding. By handpicking each stone and personalizing it with symbols, you're crafting an extension of your soul, not just forming a set. This unique connection to your tools ensures your reading is imbued with authenticity, depth, and personal power.

## Chapter 14

# The Power of the Lithomancy Chart

Traditionally, the Lithomancy Chart is a circular design, segmented into various sections. Each segment corresponds to a particular theme or aspect of life, such as love, career, health, or spiritual growth.

- **Central Circle**: This area often represents the querent (the individual seeking guidance) or the core issue/question.
- **Mid Circles** typically signify present influences, challenges, or factors affecting the central theme.
- **Outer Circles** can denote external influences, long-term outcomes, or broader themes surrounding the question.

While the above is a classic layout, the beauty of creating your own chart lies in its adaptability. You can add segments that resonate with specific areas of interest or importance in your life.

**Purpose of the Chart**

The Lithomancy Chart serves multiple purposes:

1. **Organizing Insights**: It provides a structured layout, helping decipher relationships between stones and themes.
2. **Deepening Interpretations**: You can derive deeper, layered meanings by understanding where a stone lies. For instance, when placed in the love segment, a stone symbolizing change might hint at transformations in personal relationships.
3. **Enhancing Personal Connection**: A personalized chart tailored to your life's themes and priorities can amplify resonance, making readings more intuitive and profound.

**Crafting Your Own Lithomancy Set with an Advanced Chart**

Now that you're familiar with the Lithomancy Chart let's delve into creating a harmonized set.

1. **Choose Your Stones**: Begin by selecting stones that resonate with you. These can be chosen based on their traditional meanings or personal significance. Remember, this set reflects you, so go with what feels right.
2. **Inscribe or Paint Symbols**: Consider painting or inscribing symbols on the stones if you're artistically inclined. These symbols can represent various themes or energies, adding depth to readings.
3. **Design Your Personalized Chart**: Using the traditional chart as a foundation, adapt it to your needs. You may want segments dedicated to family, personal growth, travel, or specific challenges. Use colors, symbols, or words to demarcate and decorate each section. This chart can be drawn on cloth, paper, or other surfaces.

4. **Practice with the Chart**: The real magic begins when you start practicing. Cast your stones onto the chart, noting where they land. Use the segments to derive deeper insights. For instance, if you have a stone representing courage that lands in the career segment, maybe it's time to take bold steps professionally.
5. **Evolve and Adapt**: As you grow and evolve, so should your chart. Adjust segments, add new stones, or even redesign it entirely based on where you are in life.

Creating your own lithomancy set, augmented with a personalized Lithomancy Chart, is a deeply spiritual journey and an artistic and introspective one. This melding of the mystical with the personal creates a beautiful and powerful tool. As you walk this path, remember that while traditions offer guidance, your personal touch, intuition, and experience truly bring the magic to life.

**Delving Deeper with the Lithomancy Chart**
**Why Use the Chart?**

1. **Layered Insights**: The chart helps interpret readings at multiple levels, adding dimensionality to insights.
2. **Focused Readings**: It allows the lithomancer to ask specific questions related to life areas, honing in on precise guidance.
3. **Contextual Understanding**: The chart's structure helps place each stone's energy in the context of life themes, offering a holistic view.

Harnessing the full power of the Lithomancy Chart demands a synergy of technique, intuition, and understanding. Here's how to tap into its potential:

1. **Segmented Queries**: Instead of general questions, frame queries related to the chart's segments. For instance, if you seek guidance on romantic matters, focus your intention on the chart's 'love' segment before casting the stones. The resultant pattern within that section will offer targeted insights.
2. **Inter-Relationships**: Observe the positions of stones relative to each segment. A stone related to 'career' landing in the 'relationship' segment might hint at how your professional life influences your personal relationships.
3. **Stone Pathways**: Look for patterns that traverse multiple segments. A chain of stones connecting 'health,' 'mental well-being,' and 'spirituality' could suggest a holistic approach to well-being is needed.
4. **Central Energies**: The center of the chart typically represents the querent or the primary energy. Stones that gravitate towards the center could highlight fundamental issues or overarching themes.
5. **Boundary Insights**: Stones that linger on the boundaries between segments offer dual insights. For instance, a stone on the cusp of 'family' and 'finances' might point towards financial decisions impacting family dynamics.
6. **Combining Energies**: Often, multiple stones within a segment combine their energies, offering compound insights. For example, suppose stones representing 'change' and 'growth' converge in the 'career' segment. In that case, it might signal evolving job responsibilities or a shift in your professional trajectory.
7. **Depth Over Spread**: Instead of trying to interpret every stone, focus on the most prominent patterns or stones that stand out. Sometimes, a single, prominent

stone's position can unlock deeper insights than a broader overview.

**Personalizing Your Lithomancy Chart**

While there are standard charts available, crafting a personalized chart attuned to your energies can enhance readings:

1. **Custom Segments**: Add segments that resonate with your unique journey. Whether it's 'travel,' 'learning,' or 'self-discovery,' personalize the chart to mirror your life.
2. **Evolving Layout**: As you grow and evolve, so should your chart. Regularly update it, adding, merging, or redefining segments to stay aligned with your path.
3. **Incorporate Symbols**: Infuse your chart with symbols, colors, or words with personal significance, further amplifying its resonance.

By integrating the advanced techniques of the Lithomancy Chart, practitioners can delve deeper, unlocking layers of wisdom and guidance previously obscured. Trust in its wisdom, but more importantly, trust in your intuition, and let the stones illuminate your path.

## Chapter 15

## Stones in the Stream of Life

Case studies and legitimate information are hard to source usually because it's related to sensitive information, emotions, and your client's personal details. But here, let's look at the practicalities of stone divination because, from learning about others' experiences, we are set to gain a lot.

### Stone Stories: Real-life Resonance

Most case studies and stories remain confidential to protect client privacy. However, on speaking with a local Spanish lithomancy diviner, some stories have been shared, although the names have been changed, and our source remains incognito. This shows how important it is to be sensitive to client details, how much respect practitioners have for their clients, and how to maintain a reputable business. It is not easy to access case study details. When you create your own, you will be bound by a silence that keeps your reputation intact and anchors the trust between you and your client.

**Haiden's Voyage**

Haiden sought the help of a local stone diviner in Spain during her holiday. He had been recommended to her in a local bar, and she had difficulty deciding about a love interest she had known for several months. She felt they had known each other before, possibly in a previous life, and sensed a true soul connection. After partaking in a stone reading, some interesting things came up. A cluster of planet stones indicated chaos and travel or a big move.

The love stone showed up in a past life connection regarding her love life. These were the two major components from the reading that helped her to decide on future travel plans and whether to anchor in this love relationship. The reading gave her clarity and the confidence to know that what she was moving toward was right for her.

**Jessie's Chronicle**

Jessie struggled to access her spiritual gifts and had previous visions and unpleasant encounters with spirits as a child. She had gone for several years without seeing an apparition. Finally, she came to live in an apartment without spiritual activity. After a year of being there and having no attachment to religion, she began seeing visions of Jesus Christ. She called on a local Spanish spiritualist to discuss what she was experiencing. They decided that a lithomancy reading could be helpful to see if they could uncover anything that might help her make sense of what was happening. The stones showed she was blocking her spiritual gifts and had medium abilities trying to come through. As scary as it was, she was grateful for the vision of the future and the knowledge that she could begin to take ownership of her abilities instead of them taking ownership of her.

**Avery's Saga**

Avery was having big problems with unwanted visitors of a spiritual nature. Her cats would go trance-like and stare into the middle of the room for hours, while her 2 dogs would bark as if someone was standing in front of them. There was no peace in her life. With the help of a local Spanish diviner, she created and set up a crystal grid for unwanted visitors and started 3 monthly readings. Some issues in past relationships needed cleansing, so she was recommended to a spiritual cleanser or exorcist who began cleansing her without cutting cords. The cutting of cords is not useful, as it means the soul has to go through the life lesson again, so the bad experience keeps occurring. Avery took this guidance and help for over a year, greatly impacting her mental well-being and overall health. On her last visit, she had not seen a ghost for twelve months and maintained regular readings to keep her home on an even keel.

**Sara's Expedition**

Sara was working a regular nine-to-five job in a hotel and coming home each night to create her own business as an entrepreneur. She was a single mom with huge financial responsibilities and two children to take care of. It was virtually impossible seeing a way forward. She earned a good salary at the hotel, but that only gave her the weekends to work in her business. She never took a day of rest and became overweight and stressed. There wasn't enough time to focus on her work and get it off the ground. She found all she had done was create another weekend job, not a business. She sought the help of a lithomancy stone diviner. So tired because she was always working she became obsessed with time. When was the right time for her business to fly? Why won't it happen now? After a stone reading, she found two stones predicted a few months ahead when new beginnings would be rewarded. She saw that she still had one foot in the past and needed to keep looking forward to reaching her business goals. The stones gave her a window of a few weeks where it would benefit her to make some big decisions. She was ready and felt ready. The reading gave her clarity and confidence to move forward at the right time.

## The Diviner's Diary

Talking to a local Spanish Stone diviner gives us enormous insights into how one ordinary man can see the benefits of foretelling with stones for many people in the spiritual community.

People often think that looking into the future is negative, associated with witchcraft, spirits, and ghosts. These opinions are reserved for people who don't understand spirituality and have no experience. From talking with lithomancy experts, it's clear that this type of personal investigation and personal development allows many people to create a map to plan their future ideas and dreams. Over the last 15 years expert I spoke with has seen huge transformational changes in the clients he has worked with. He has helped women start families who believed they could never have children. He has worked with business people struggling financially to move away from living on the breadline to becoming successful business owners, and he has also mentored and coached fellow spiritual Souls into their spiritual businesses. This has been beneficial for his business and enabled the growth of his success while supporting newcomers to the spiritual scene.

This kind of work comes through the heart space. It is work that is undertaken with dedication and love. It has no set working pattern or standard working hours and is a type of work you can do anywhere in the world. However, it should be noted that the Pagan roots of this type of work can sometimes make it unpopular where spiritualism is not a common practice. But in Western society, spiritualism has become very popular. It is increasing in popularity as it benefits those who enjoy self-exploration and self-development, free from religion's fixed writings and instructions, for those who want a more open and fluid approach to Faith and its meanings.

One story of personal transformation is the story of Rachel. She discovered that lithomancy could help her by accident through her organic passion for collecting crystals. She wore crystals regularly because of the energetic transaction she received from wearing the gemstone jewelry. After some time, she realized that her energy wouldn't feel the same when she wasn't wearing her crystals, so she regularly turned to her crystal jewelry for support. She felt that crystals gave her emotional protection, especially when she was going into the city, where she would feel lots of different energies, which would be hard for her to manage.

Rachel is an empath and finds handling other people's energy around her challenging. Scared minerals have given her the strength to retain her energy in busy settings such as parties, workplaces, and even with friends at simple gatherings. By chance, she was recommended to a stone diviner by her business coach, a spiritualist. Rachel began to take regular readings and was quietly surprised by the results. Over time, she could see that the stones indicated times when she could make better decisions in her life, and they also supported her in explaining where she had made poor choices. She began to understand elements of her past lives and how they affected the decisions she made in this life. She had been in a toxic relationship for many years, not understanding the soul contract she had made, and this began a process of unpacking why she chose bad relationships.

Rachel's world began to open up, and she studied her past lives and soul contracts, which she had never fully understood. The spiritual world was now opening up in ways she had never imagined, and it felt like peeling an onion; whenever she removed a layer, another layer appeared. Some of the work was painful, and she sometimes felt like giving up. There were also times when she got sick, and the work was too emotional. However, it didn't seem to matter how many times there were bumps in the road. She was always drawn back to her rocks and crystals and the support they gave her. She decided to go deeper into understanding the energetic transaction made between crystals on human beings, and she was surprised by what she learned. Her knowledge of rocks, minerals, and crystals gradually deepened, and she began to study the sacred art of stone divining.

Rachel began stone casting for herself, and her readings were basic and confusing for many months. She kept a diary of all her findings, hoping to get clarity around all the information she was recording. She began to see patterns in her life. Her spiritual gifts grew as she continued healing and working with spiritual mentors. Unknowingly, she developed a way to communicate with souls that had passed to the other side.

She never believed that something like this was possible for her. Having had premonitions as a child and seeing ghosts growing up, she always knew she was a little different. Still, she could never tap into that side of her on demand. She felt helpless and unable to access her higher self when she wanted to. Her true self seemed to show up when she suffered emotionally or excitedly. From day to day, accessing that part of her being was very hard.

As more time passed, her stone-defining work opened up her intuition. She started casting using her intuition as a guide and her heart chakra when asking the stones questions. At the beginning of her practice, and after building confidence in her stone readings, she offered lithomancy to her friends and family. Initially, she wanted to compare her readings to readings to see if she could learn anything different, and this steadily developed her confidence in her spiritual ability. She began to see wild differences between her and other people's readings, which made her realize that foretelling with stones was not a joke. These readings were as unique as every human being, and there was so much to be learned from every reading she just did.

Her friends were also pleasantly surprised that they could foretell moments in their future and start to make plans and develop them in new ways. Rachel continued to practice on herself and with her friends and family, which grew her confidence slowly. She recorded all her findings and created case studies to look back on and learn from.

Today Rachel continues to practice lithomancy for herself and in her spiritual business. While she cannot talk about her clients and preserves complete confidentiality, she has been open to discussing her journey and sharing the successes and joys of her own business. Readings are just part of her spiritual business. Now she is a fully-fledged medium and believes this is all due to the few precious stones she started casting many years ago.

It's hard to believe that stone divining can open the door for other spiritual gifts. But a new door opens when you begin tapping into your intuition and trusting yourself, listening for the answers inside your body rather than the words coming from your mind. This is the first time anyone knows where this kind of work can take you, and spiritual work often evolves continuously over the years from one level to the next.

If you love rocks and crystals, this will denote a special connection to the energetic properties held by these amazing pieces of earth. Suppose one person can practice lithomancy and make it a successful part of their life and business. In that case, that is something open for exploration and available for you too. Just imagine how exciting it would be to work in a business you loved. Never felt like work. People regarded you highly and respected you.

## Practical Pebbles: Lithomancy in the Living

Stone divination in daily life remains a practice mainly used by foretellers of the future, namely those with a love or connection to stone and crystals. Many crystal experts use their gemstones deeply and meaningfully for their crystal practice or business.

Stones are still used in many pagan practices that have become mainstream, such as a stone blessing at a wedding, where stones are given to each guest, who then holds and blesses them throughout the sacred ritual.

Stones are used in health and welling settings, mainly in décor and stone massage. While that doesn't refer to lithomancy directly, it relies on the stone's energetic vibration and weight to assist massage and work with pressure points and meridians of the body.

Again, not directly divination, but gemstones, crystal, and rocks are all worn in jewelry, increasing in popularity as time passes. Certain gemstones make us feel good or have a significant meaning, bringing us back to the symbolism and meaning of rocks.

Stone divination is primarily used for reading and to foretell the future. These practices are run personally by practitioners and vary in style from one master to another. Always research when choosing a spiritual guide, and ensure their type of stone divination resonates and aligns with you. If they come recommended, then that's a plus point too!

## Navigating the Lithomancy Labyrinth

As you open up your sacred portal and awaken your spiritual gifts, you'll find that there will be some bumps in the road. This journey has no destination and no end point! It's continual, sacred, healing, enlightening, and powerful; it's good to remember that every day.

Those souls embarking on spiritual awakening don't choose it because it's easy. And I say the word, choose with trepidation! You've probably felt along your life's path that you have a higher calling or receive wisdom and knowledge in a way that others don't. You don't choose this; it is part of you and forms what is. Maybe you feel things more deeply or others' energy so much that it's changed the trajectory of your life. Even if you haven't, don't worry! Your spirit, calling, higher self, god-self, or whatever you want to name it, is inside you. It's inside everyone. Some of us open it up early, some don't, and there is no right or wrong way. This notion can cause problems with your feelings and understanding and problems with your family and friends. Don't expect to be understood or respected for your choices. And that's okay. Your dream is not someone else's; therefore, we can't expect another soul to understand or appreciate it. It will take time to find your tribe, and you may never find a tribe. That doesn't matter, but this is your journey, and the right pieces will unfold before you once you begin. Instead of feeling the burden of these issues, see them as beautiful challenges you will face to increase your spiritual growth and, ultimately, your power in stone divination.

There may be practical challenges in lithomancy too. There will likely be times when you don't understand how to interpret the stones, which will evolve with repeated practice and time. Always record your findings and the places where you get stuck. Ask others for help, especially in your niche, as they can guide and steer you on the right path. Getting a spiritual mentor to guide, coach, and co-pilot your journey is especially helpful. We often get lost and stuck in our thoughts; a gentle push or redirection is needed.

Also, we've discussed intuition and how to guide yourself in your lithomancy practice. Looking and seeking answers will always be your first port of call, but you must learn to trust yourself. Intuition is also something that develops over time, too don't try to rush it or fake it. Everything comes at its right and perfect time. No journey ever worth taking is easy.

# Conclusion

For some of us, how we think about time allows us to divine or map out the future. Suppose we can see forward, into time and space, and predict the months that reflect prosperity or find the right season to change our lives. In that case, it helps us take control of our existence and creation.

Beginning your practice in lithomancy will expand your mind into multi-dimensions. You will open, and close portals, and the magic and mystery of life's wonders will start to unfold. You will begin to experience levels of evolution; every time you reach a new level, another one will appear. This is your spiritual growth. This is your intuition. These are your celestial gifts. Getting stronger by the day. Every client you read for will be an opportunity for learning and growth. All the experience you have, both good and bad, will push you towards mastery. Nothing in this journey will be easy, but nothing worth doing ever is.

You're on your path to your life's purpose, in stone divination, a fledgling lithomancer! You have everything you need to become a lithomancy diviner, and the journey starts here.

This book has taken you on a journey. One you didn't think would be possible when you started out. But now your introduction to lithomancy is complete. What parts stood out to you?

# Conclusion

Because that small flame that's ignited in you is usually where you'll begin. It would help if you scratched or a flicker of excitement when you get an itch. This sparks a journey. Journeying into the spiritual field isn't always easy. You'll come across those who have different beliefs from you. You'll meet those with huge egos that appear to be spiritually superior. And you'll also meet those with hearts the size of the ocean, operating from a space of love in the heart chakra. They will, metaphorically speaking, take you in and under their wing. They'll share the riches of spirituality with you, guide, encourage, and support you even on your darkest days. Those are the golden friends you should hold on to and listen to. The spiritual field is just like any other community or religion. There is a diverse and divergent mix of souls.

There will be times when you feel like giving up and throwing in the towel. Sometimes things won't make sense, and you'll try three, four, or even five times, and they still won't make sense! The universe has a funny way of sending us messages, slowing us down, and then speeding us up when all the planets are aligned for us. Everything will come at the right time. And if you're unsure, do your own stone casting to see what planetary alignment is occurring and how this impacts you. If you've come this far and feel a connection to lithomancy, it's aligned for you. It's just up to you to begin deepening and developing your intuition.

Why is intuition so important? We can discuss intuition until the cows come home, and you know by now just how important it is to develop your intuition, to make your spiritual work a success. Not only that, but it's also important for you to work within your life's purpose because this is where your intuition will take you. Dreams and abundance activate when living in this space. All the talk about manifestation activates when calling in your intuition and acting on it. It's not a joke that luck comes to some people and not others. It comes to those who practice the good deeds bestowed to them from their intuition, nothing more. And you can apply all these findings and gifts to your lithomancy practice.

## Conclusion

You'll see how important it is as you practice developing your intuition. The more you do it, the more divine inspiration you'll receive. Always make time to nourish and grow it.

As we continue to conclude, let's reflect upon your style of stone divination. Remember, it's not vital to have a steadfast ritual in place. Be flexible. Let your client feel into the stones and see what they're attracted to. It's often very useful to allow your client to spend a few minutes with the stones, allowing the stones to feel your client's vibration and energy so the minerals can do their magic work. This will make your job a lot easier too. And in the same vein, don't let your client take advantage of you. Ensure you are clear with appointment times, and don't let anyone push boundaries. Things like this happen easily in the spiritual field because soft emotions are deeply evoked in both parties.

Always remember to offer your readings as a guide. Don't make promises you cannot keep or be overconfident when you are not so sure. Be authentic, be you, and keep learning. That's where your professionalism and success will lie. Sometimes, the work of spiritual souls gets a bad rap, and unscrupulous practitioners tarnish everyone else in the community with a bad name through bad practices. There will always be ups and downs but do not feed into poor practices and operations. Always hold your standards high and treat your work like its legitimate business.

Self-reflection will be a huge part of maintaining a business in stone divination that grows and flourishes. And this also brings us to why self-reflection is so important in foretelling with stones.

Stone divination helps us see past versions of ourselves and our past lives. And these allow us to make sense of our world. Many souls in the spiritual realm have felt a connection to something else since they were children. Perhaps having deep-seated memories and flickers of experiences, they can't explain. These stories or visions of ourselves help us understand our behavior in this lifetime. We often seek answers to questions we know nothing about and look for logic or reasons why we made terrible mistakes

## Conclusion

or poor decisions. The human brain always wants to work things out and find reasons, even when there are none.

But this area of self-reflection is healthy and provides a sense of understanding and calm for us and our clients. We move forward by being aware of previous mistakes and avoiding repeating them. Lithomancy is a great helping hand, as we can easily look at the past. What stones connect in this area, and does it provide a link to the present or the future? What can it tell us to see or avoid? This reflection is extremely helpful in today's busy and brutal life. Self-reflection is a way of nurturing ourselves. Those that do not understand may think of your practice as hocus-pocus. Still, you are taking great strides in the wellness space and giving people the support and clarity they need.

Lithomancy has supreme power in the areas of personal growth. As humans, we seek to understand ourselves. We are desperate to understand who we are, why we're here, and our motives! This lifetime is not easy, and finding answers takes a lot of work. Some of us come into this world into families facing hardship and trauma, unable to see the wood for the trees. Some clients may not have talked to a spiritual guide or a counselor. This may be the first kind of self-exploration they have undertaken. What an honor it is to help someone along their journey. To guide, motivate and explain the findings along their path. This is work done from the heart space, and it will be exhausting. Spiritual work always is. Calling in and attuning our third eye, our intuition takes work, and you will need a lot of rest. You've never used this sixth sense before. Feeling like this is completely normal.

Personal growth helps others achieve fulfillment. And where you have happy, fulfilled clients, you will create the business of your dreams. Never trivialize the work that you do. It is super important and strongly needed in this day and age. Misguidance is everywhere, notably through our television screens and smartphones, but it's everywhere. Being part of the conscious collective trying to help others reach a higher standard in themselves must

## Conclusion

be rewarded and reveled in. This is your job! This is what you do! This is your higher calling!

The beauty and popularity of lithomancy stone divination is simply because it provides clarity. In life, we are constantly faced with challenges. We fight battles that are not our own and take on problems that don't belong to us. Lithomancy helps us see what is for us to deal with and what is not. This way, we can make better decisions and live our fullest lives.

This is also a way to reach your truest desires. And ultimately, that's what we all want. To obtain the things we truly seek in life. Lithomancy helps us to get there. Supporting, explaining, guiding, and shining a light along the true path.

Your lithomancy work is valuable to the community at large. Helping others to make better decisions and gain clarity in their lives. It is a reputable business that you can grow and create from and help others find fulfillment and true satisfaction for yourself.

# REFERENCES

Besnier, D. M. (n.d.). Mesopotamian Divination: A world full of signs – Esagil Games. Esagil Games. Retrieved June 17, 2023, from https://esagil.co.uk/mesopotamia-the-land-between-the-rivers/mesopotamian-divination-a-world-full-of-signs/#:~:text=Mesopotamian%20divination%20is%20a%20lot

Biointernational, C. (2022, May 17). Essential Oils for Spiritual Awakening | Best Oils for Spiritual Connection. VedaOils. https://www.vedaoils.com/blogs/essentialoils/essential-oils-for-spiritual-awakening

Ceridwen. (2022, July 24). Lithomancy: Full Beginner's Guide to Casting Stones With Free Chart - Craft of Wicca. Craftofwicca.com. https://craftofwicca.com/lithomancy-full-beginners-guide-to-casting-stones-with-free-chart/

Dachinger, D. (2013, June 24). Lithomancy, the Psychic Art of Reading Stones: Gary L. Wimmer Explains The Fascinating Art Of Divination Through Lithomancy. Www.newswire.com. https://www.newswire.com/news/lithomancy-the-psychic-art-of-reading-stones-gary-l-wimmer-explains-the-11181

Eyre, S. (2019, October 13). Reading Stones. Susan Eyre. https://susaneyre.blog/2019/10/13/reading-stones/

Gann, K. (2010, February 10). Kyle Gann: The Planets. Www.kylegann.com. https://www.kylegann.com/Planets.html#:~:text=And%20since%20Mercury%20is%20a

Gazur, B. (2022, December 27). 10 Important Religious Rocks and Stones. Listverse. https://listverse.com/2022/12/27/10-important-religious-rocks-and-stones/

Hall, J. (2012, February). Positive Health Online | Article - Scrying - Using Crystals for Guidance and Well-Being. Www.positivehealth.com. https://www.positivehealth.com/article/crystal-healing/scrying-using-crystals-for-guidance-and-well-being

Hewitt, D. G. (2019, January 2). Birds, Entrails and Newborn Babies: 20 of the Strangest Fortune Telling Methods from History. History Collection. https://historycollection.com/birds-entrails-and-newborn-babies-20-of-the-strangest-fortune-telling-methods-from-history/9/

Hickley, K. (2015, March 13). A Sage Smudging Ritual To Cleanse Your Aura & Clear Your Space. Mindbodygreen. https://www.mindbodygreen.com/articles/smudging-101-burning-sage

How to Activate My Crystal Sphere? | Village Rock Shop. (n.d.). Www.villagerockshop.com; Village Rock Shop. Retrieved July 2, 2023, from https://www.villagerockshop.com/faqs/how-to-activate-my-crystal-sphere/#:~:text=Clear%20crystals%20work%20well%20with

How to Spot Fake Crystals. (n.d.). Crystals Rock Australia; Crystals Rock Australia.

# References

https://www.crystalsrock.com.au/blogs/crystals-rock-blog/how-to-spot-fake-crystals

Kedia, S. (2020, April 10). Spiritual Symbols | 31 Common Spiritual Symbols and Meanings. TheMindFool - Perfect Medium for Self-Development & Mental Health. Explorer of Lifestyle Choices & Seeker of the Spiritual Journey. https://themindfool.com/spiritual-symbols/

King, Hobart. M. (n.d.). Gems from Space! Peridot Moldavite Tektite Desert Glass. Geology.com. Retrieved June 29, 2023, from https://geology.com/gemstones/gems-from-space/#:~:text=Pallasites%20are%20stony%2Diron%20meteorites

Leavy, A. (2017, January 25). Lithomancy: Casting Stones to Read the Future - Love & Light School of Crystal Therapy. loveandlightschool.com. https://loveandlightschool.com/lithomancy-casting-stones-to-read-the-future/

Lotus Vs. Water Lilies, What's The Difference? (2017, April 30). Container Water Gardens; Container Water Gardens. https://www.containerwatergardens.net/lotus-vs-water-lilies-whats-difference/

Marsden, A. (2020, January 26). Prayer Pebbles & Praying Stones | Salem Chapel, Martin Top. Martintop.org.uk. https://martintop.org.uk/blog/prayer-pebbles-praying-stones

Mcdermott, T. (2018, August 10). One Way I Do Crystal Readings. Www.youtube.com. https://www.youtube.com/watch?v=XbBzG7MY93E

Medieval Era. (n.d.). Medieval Times Dinner & Tournament. https://www.medievaltimes.com/education/medieval-era#:~:text=The%20medieval%20era%2C%20often%20called

Ponder, W. (2022, February 5). Divination With Crystals: How To Use Crystals For Divination And Fortune-Telling. Mystic Crystal Imports. https://mysticcrystalimports.com/blogs/crystals/divination-with-crystals-how-to-use-crystals-for-divination-and-fortune-telling

Said, M. (2018, December). Mesopotamian Magic in the First Millennium B.C. Metmuseum.org. https://www.metmuseum.org/toah/hd/magic/hd_magic.htm

Selby-Gius, D. (n.d.). crystal grid - Crystal Enhancements. Crystalenhancements.com. Retrieved July 2, 2023, from https://crystalenhancements.com/?s=crystal+grid

Selby-Gius, D. (2021, December 30). Crystal Enhancements Welcomes You! Crystalenhancements.com. https://crystalenhancements.com/

Stewart, T. (2021, October 17). Step By Step: How to Cleanse A Space (Energetically & Spiritually). Whimsy Soul. https://whimsysoul.com/how-to-cleanse-a-space-energetically-and-spiritually/

Thomas, A. A. (2022, August 18). Rare Knuckle Bones Engraved With Names Of Gods And Used In Divination Discovered In Ancient City. Zenger News. https://www.zenger.news/2022/08/18/rare-knuckle-bones-engraved-with-names-of-gods-and-used-in-divination-discovered-in-ancient-city/

Ward, K. (2021, March 29). You Can Find Out if You'll Fall in Love by Throwing

# References

Your Favorite Crystals. Cosmopolitan. https://www.cosmopolitan.com/lifestyle/a35971153/crystal-fortune-telling/

We'Moon. (n.d.). Full and New Moon Rituals—Intention Setting and Actualization. We'Moon. Retrieved July 2, 2023, from https://wemoon.ws/blogs/magical-arts/full-and-new-moon-rituals#:~:text=Full%20Moon%20Rituals%20are%20generally

wiccanery. (n.d.). Lithomancy. Tumblr; Micaela. Retrieved June 26, 2023, from https://wiccanery.tumblr.com/post/187467917627/lithomancy

Wimmer, G. (2014). Lithomancy the Psychic Art of Reading Stones. Lithomancy.com. http://lithomancy.com/

Wimmer, G. (2023a, April 5). Lithomancy Explained. Www.youtube.com. https://www.youtube.com/watch?v=4SaX84suM7w

Wimmer, G. (2023b, April 19). LITHOMANCY: The Psychic Art of Reading Stones | LIVE READING by NDEr Gary Wimmer. Www.youtube.com. https://www.youtube.com/watch?v=5WbUWkBGZnE

Wimmer, G. L. (2011). Lithomancy, the Psychic Art of Reading Stones. Createspace Independent Pub.

# About the Author

**Monique Joiner Siedlak: Author, Witch, Warrior.**

With storytelling infused with mysticism, modern paganism, and new age spirituality, Monique awakens your potential. Initiated into the craft at 20, her 80+ books explore the magick and mysteries of life.

A Long Island native, she now calls Southeast Poland home but remains a citizen of Mother Earth.

Beyond her pen, Monique craves new experiences and cherishes nature, advocating for animal welfare.

Join her captivating journey as she transports you to enchanting realms and empowers your own transformative path. Unleash the dormant magic within and embrace the extraordinary with Monique Joiner Siedlak's evocative words.

To find out more about Monique artistically, spiritually, and personally, feel free to visit her **official website**.

www.mojosiedlak.com

- facebook.com/mojosiedlak
- twitter.com/mojosiedlak
- instagram.com/mojosiedlak
- youtube.com/@MoniqueJoinerSiedlak_Author
- tiktok.com/@mojosiedlak
- bookbub.com/authors/monique-joiner-siedlak
- pinterest.com/mojosiedlak

**African Spirituality Beliefs and Practices**
Hoodoo
Seven African Powers: The Orishas
Cooking for the Orishas
Lucumi: The Ways of Santeria
Voodoo of Louisiana
Haitian Vodou
Orishas of Trinidad
Connecting with your Ancestors
Blood Magick
The Orishas
Vodun: West Africa's Spiritual Life
Marie Laveau: Life of a Voodoo Queen
Candomblé: Dancing for the God
Umbanda
Exploring the Rich and Diverse World

**The Elemental Magic Series**
Wiccan Basics
Candle Magick
Wiccan Spells
Love Spells
Abundance Spells
Herb Magick
Moon Magick
Creating Your Own Spells
Gypsy Magic
Protection Magick
Celtic Magick
Shamanic Magick
Crystal Magic

**The Spiritual Empowerment Series**
Creative Visualization

# More Books by Monique

Astral Projection for Beginners
Meditation for Beginners
Reiki for Beginners
Manifesting With the Law of Attraction
Time Bound
Healing Animals with Reiki
Being an Empath Today
Crystal Healing
Communicating with Your Spirit Guides

**Life on Fire**
Healing Your Inner Child
Change Your Life
Raising Your Vibe

**Get a Handle on Life**
Get a Handle on Stress
Get a Handle on Anxiety
Get a Handle on Depression
Get a Handle on Procrastination

**The Holistic Yoga and Wellness Series**
Yoga for Beginners
Yoga for Stress
Yoga for Back Pain
Yoga for Weight Loss
Yoga for Flexibility
Yoga for Advanced Beginners
Yoga for Fitness
Yoga for Runners
Yoga for Energy
Yoga for Your Sex Life
Yoga to Beat Depression and Anxiety
Yoga for Menstruation
Yoga to Detox Your Body

MORE BOOKS BY MONIQUE

Yoga to Tone Your Body

**The DIY Body Care Series**
Creating Your Own Body Butter
Creating Your Own Body Scrub
Creating Your Own Body Spray

# SUPPORT ME BY LEAVING A REVIEW!

## goodreads

www.ingramcontent.com/pod-product-compliance
Lightning Source LLC
Chambersburg PA
CBHW060835050426
42453CB00008B/707